Let's Write! Grades 4-6

Reading, Writing, Thinking, Spelling and Grammar Activities to Promote Creative Expression

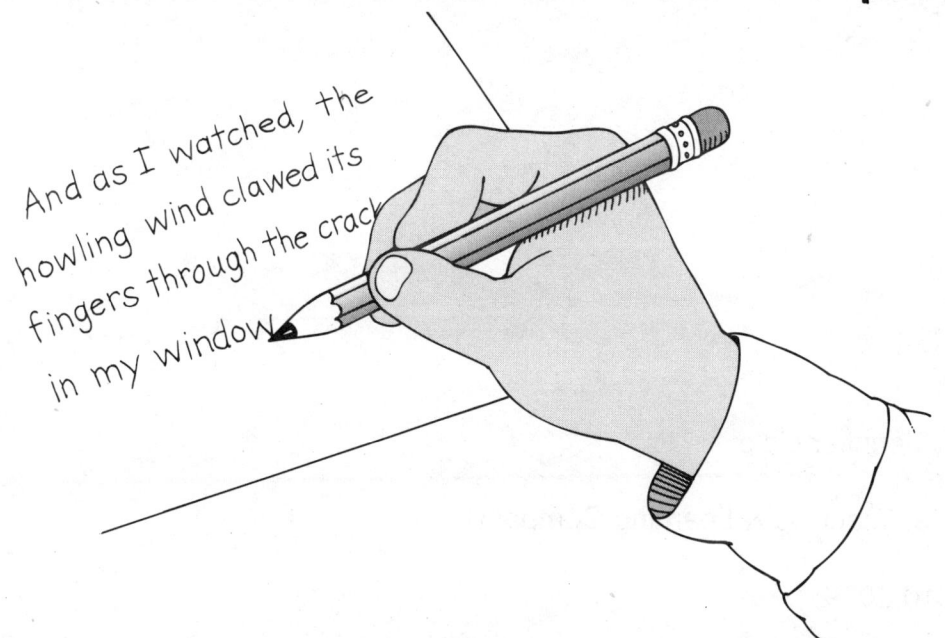

And as I watched, the howling wind clawed its fingers through the crack in my window

Robynne Eagan and Tracey Ann Schofield
Illustrated by Darcy Tom

Teaching & Learning Company
1204 Buchanan St., P.O. Box 10
Carthage, IL 62321-0010

Cover design by Jennifer Little

Copyright © 1999, Teaching & Learning Company

ISBN No. 1-57310-203-2

Printing No. 987654321

**Teaching & Learning Company
1204 Buchanan St., P.O. Box 10
Carthage, IL 62321-0010**

The purchase of this book entitles teachers to make copies for use in their individual classrooms only. This book, or any part of it, may not be reproduced in any form for any other purposes without prior written permission from the Teaching & Learning Company. It is strictly prohibited to reproduce any part of this book for an entire school or school district, or for commercial resale.

All rights reserved. Printed in the United States of America.

This book belongs to

_____

Dedications

To the next generation of writers: they are our creative hope.

Tracey

To my grandmothers: Edith Cochrane and Elizabeth Johnson, for all of the stories over the years.

Robynne

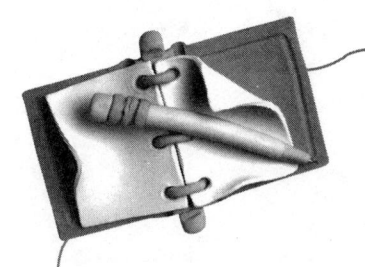

Table of

Assess and Evaluate 7
Observing and Assessing Young
    Writers 8
Student Self-Assessment 9
Sharing 10

Chapter 1
The Purpose of Print

Reading and Writing Are Part of
    Our World 12
How Did It All Start? 13
In the Beginning 14
International Symbols 15
The Origins of Writing 16

Chapter 2
For the Love of Language

Oral Language Experience 18
Strategies to Get Young Writers
    Excited About Writing 19
Copycats 20
She's So Nice 22
The Angry Alphabet 24
The "No-No" Game 25
Flights of Fancy 26
Metaphorically Speaking 28
Metaphor Madness 29
Word Wizards 31
Synonym Sound-Alikes 32

Poetry Primer 34
Rhyme Around 34
Fun with Free Verse 36
Couplet Capers 37
Haiku 38
Plain Cinquain 39
The Five Ws Poem 40

Chapter 3: The Right Stuff

Let's Write! .42
Getting Started 42
Timed Writing 43
Treasure Chest 44
Unlock Your Imagination 45
Don't Miss a Thing 46
Silly Sentences 47
Silly Sentences Flip-Up Book 48
Silly Sentences Sample Grid 49
Playing with Paragraphs 50
Brainstorming 53
Clustering .54
Tree Cluster 55
The Writing Process 56
Editing 57
Editing Center 58
The Goof-Proof Grammar Guide 59

Contents

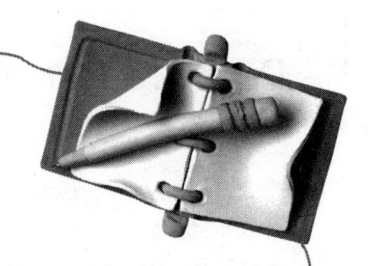

Chapter 4: Write for a Reason

I Love Lists 62
How'd He Do That? 64
How'd He Do That? Model Activity 65
Write a Letter 66
Informal Letter Sample 67
Formal Letter Sample 68
Research and Report 69
Writing a Report 69
Research and Report Checklist 71
Genres 72
Write a Children's Book 73
Get to Know a Writer 74

Chapter 5: Story Makers

Say It Your Own Way 76
Story Builders 77
Story Starters 78
Story Starters List 79
What a Character! 80
Frankenstein's Monster Character
    Sketch .81
Easy Epithets 81
Knock Knock. Who's There? 82
From the Outside In 83
Dr. Jeckle and Mr. Hyde: An Alter
    Ego Exercise 84
Descriptive Obits 85
Point of View: Who's Story Is This? . . .86

1st, 2nd, 3rd . . . and 4th 89
Choosing a Setting 91
Repetition .92
Stacking 93
Getting Tense 94
Past, Present and Future 96
Look Who's Talking 97
To Whom Am I Speaking? 99
Paper Arguments 100
Back Talk 101
All Good Things Must Come to
    an End 102
Title Tricks 104

Chapter 6
Let's Have Some Fun

Come to Your Senses 108
The Movie Name Game 110
The Brave Heart of Patch Adams:
    A Movie Title Story Starter 111
Let's Do Lunch 112

Appendix

Grade 4 Writing Assessment Form . . .118
Grade 5 Writing Assessment Form . . .121
Grade 6 Writing Assessment Form . . .124
Writing Tips for Aspiring Authors 127
Answer Key 128

Dear Teacher or Parent,

Children love language. As educators, we can nurture this natural affinity and augment it with an understanding of the mechanics of written expression to help children to become enthusiastic, motivated and competent writers. But the real magic begins when we sprinkle a liberal dose of creative inspiration over the common curriculum and kids begin to put words on paper—not because they have to write, but because they want to write!

Stock up on paper and keep those pencils sharp; *Let's Write! Grades 4-6* will have students writing—and loving it!

This third book in the innovative *Let's Write!* series for children is filled with intriguing and educational activities that will help students to become enthusiastic and productive writers. Designed to increase the students' love of writing while developing communication skills and encouraging freedom of expression, *Let's Write! Grades 4-6* familiarizes children with the writing process and helps remove obstacles to creativity. Using a variety of teacher-directed and independent curriculum-based creative writing exercises, this invaluable resource supports educators in their development of a technically comprehensive and stimulating writing program that promotes reading, writing, creative thinking, spelling and grammatical accuracy and broadens oral and written language literacy skills.

Let's Write! Grades 4-6 introduces children to the fundamentals of written expression and gives students the skills and the confidence they need to become successful and motivated writers. By promoting a creative learning environment and using tools such as *Let's Write!* to foster a love of language, educators are giving children a gift that lasts a lifetime.

Each book in the Let's Write! series is designed to expose young writers to the wonder of words and the magic of language. The books, which provide educators with a collection of exciting activities that introduce and expand on reading, writing and expressive concepts for three targeted developmental levels, can stand alone as creative writing units or be used in combination to supplement the language curriculum.

Sincerely,

Robynne Tracey

Robynne Eagan and Tracey Ann Schofield

Assess and Evaluate

Language encompasses reading, writing and oral and visual communication. Evaluation and assessment should be regarded as extensions of the writing process.

Assessments and evaluations should be positive, proactive and respectful of a young writer's need to feel secure about his or her written offerings–even if they need work!

Assessment

Assess young writers through an informal process of ongoing observation that monitors progress through predictable stages of development and a predetermined set of skill expectations. Prescribed resources, assessment criteria and professional judgment can be used to assess a child's degree of mastery of specific knowledge and skills. Assessment provides an accurate picture of student abilities and monitors the success of a writing program.

Evaluation

Evaluation is an examination based on established curriculum expectations. Evaluation assigns a value to a student's work and abilities. This process should occur at regular intervals throughout the writing program. Evaluation data provides valuable information regarding a student's progress and the success of a writing program. This data enables educators to measure and record progress and assign grades or marks to students and information to parents and the school district.

Standardized assessment programs are designed to compare groups of children and provide a record of how particular groups and districts perform in relation to one another on a defined set of tasks in a controlled environment.

knowledge: facts, concepts, ideas, vocabulary and stories possessed and understood by an individual

skill: ability to perform a specific task that can be learned, observed and evaluated

Observing and Assessing Young Writers

Several methods can be used to systematically observe young writers. A combination of methods provides a good basis for understanding individual developmental levels. Build a repertoire of assessment tools that work for you.

Stages of Development Forms

Create a page to outline the various stages of predictable language development. Graphs, checklists or observational comments can be incorporated into this form.

Anecdotal Comments

Carry a clipboard and jot down notes, dates and observations. Transfer your observations to notebooks or personal anecdotal reporting pages. These can be used to evaluate and report a child's progress. Parents will appreciate these "snapshots" of their child in action.

Observation Checklist

Develop observation forms to be used for individuals engaged in a particular activity. Create a list of definite skills and development that you expect this activity to demonstrate and teach.

_____'s Anecdotal Report

Date	Observation

Writing Center Activity Checklist

Name: _____

Date: _____

Observations

- ❒ demonstrates skill with writing tools
- ❒ prints legibly
- ❒ demonstrates creativity in written work
- ❒ combines print and pictures to express ideas
- ❒ makes use of various strategies to spell words
- ❒ demonstrates confidence with print

Student Self-Assessment

Active student self-assessment can be a valuable part of the writing process. This exercise engages students, increases their understanding of expectations and offers further experience with the skills, knowledge and concepts being introduced and mastered.

Students must know what is expected in a work and must possess the skills needed to produce that work. Children should understand the criteria that make the work acceptable or outstanding. Students who recognize the strengths and weaknesses in a work will be better able to improve their written assignments.

How Did I Do?

1. For this assignment I am expected to:
   _____
   _____
   _____

   I did everything that was expected on this assignment.

2. My work should be:
   _____
   _____
   _____

   My work met the standards listed above.

Comments: _____
_____
_____

Sharing

A sharing classroom is a learning classroom!

The sharing of accomplishments and ideas may be the single most important factor in turning students into effective writers.

The sharing process provides intrinsic motivation and opportunities to reinforce and develop new skills. Most children are very excited to share work and will love the experience. The encouragement of and input from their peers will help them to gain confidence and develop competence. Make sharing a positive experience where children will receive reinforcement and praise from peers, educators, volunteers and parents.

Works can be shared aloud, displayed in print on bulletin boards or made available to others to read and offer comments.

Sharing reinforces new abilities, and exposure to other writing gives children the opportunity to improve their own. Develop a reading and writing culture in your class by sharing works and encouraging dialogue about challenges, ideas and accomplishments. The sharing of written works will inspire your students to be creative, thoughtful and thorough in expressing their thoughts in print.

Chapter 1

The Purpose of Print

Reading and Writing Are Part of Our World

Most of us take our written language for granted. Stop and think about it for a minute. The printed letter and number are everywhere!

Writing allows people to share thoughts, messages and information with one another. Can you imagine what the world would be like without letters and numbers?

Make a schedule that gives an overview of the things you do from the time you wake up until the time you go to bed. How is writing important in your life? How is your life affected by writing? How many of the things that you do rely on the use of letters, words and numbers?

Do you rely on the clock to tell you when it is time to go? Does your school bus rely on the clock? Would your bus driver know where to go if there weren't a schedule or map to show him the way? And what about street names and signs? How would we find our way to new places without them? School would certainly be different! Don't forget that a world without written letters and words would be a world without telephones, newspapers, computers and television. We would not be able to keep track of many things that we count on today; even a shopping list would be difficult if we couldn't write it down.

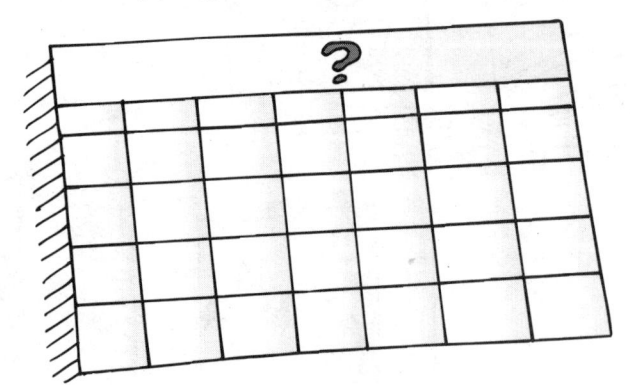

✓ What was the first word you learned how to write? How did it feel?
✓ What was the first word you learned how to read?
✓ How do words help you in your day-to-day life?
✓ How might books affect a society?

How Did It All Start?

*Why do people write? Do all people write?
Do you think that people have always used printed letters and words?
Why might people have wanted to write? How did people keep track of
important events and information before writing?*

Before print, people relied on memories and stories that had been passed from one person to the next. People spread information and entertaining stories by telling them to one another. When life was simpler and fewer details needed to be passed on, this system worked quite well.

In time, people developed systems to help them recall and record important events and information. Some people recorded their stories and information in picture form on cave walls, stone cliffs, stone tablets or animal hides. These pictures represented particular events and places that were important to the people who lived there. Unfortunately, when the people moved on, they could not take their stories with them.

North American natives recorded their stories by weaving sequences of colored shell beads into a wampum belt. The number, colors and sequence of beads represented particular details and information that the natives wanted to pass on to future generations. Native storytellers of Peru preserved their tribal stories and knowledge by using a system of colored strings and knots that formed a kind of necklace called a quipu.

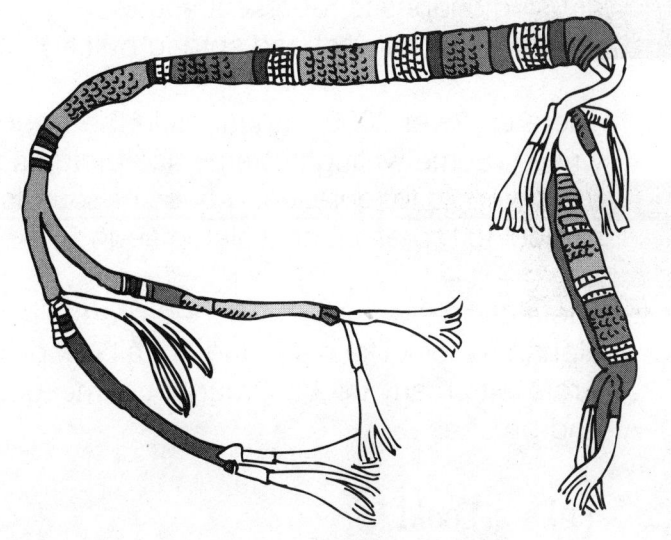

In many places around the world people have found early pictures that stand for particular objects. These pictures are called pictograms, and they are an important early step in the development of written language. Some scientists devote their lives to trying to read pictograms from long ago. When we figure out what the pictograms represent, we can learn many things about the early civilizations that left their mark so long ago.

- ✓ Find out if there are any petroglyphs in your area. Visit the site or a museum to view samples of early writing.
- ✓ Display photographs of cave drawings as shown in books, magazines and newspapers.

In the Beginning

About 10,000 years ago in the ancient region of Mesopotamia (now Iraq), people used little clay tokens with pictures of things people had to trade on them to make the exchange of goods a little easier. This code and the idea of a common printed code began to spread.

Almost 5000 years later the Ancient Sumerian people developed a faster method for making their symbols in the wet clay. They carved a wedge into the end of a stick and pressed it into wet clay. This wedge-shaped writing, called cuniform, turned the picture code into a code of printed symbols.

In time, the Sumerian symbols came to represent sounds of the language instead of particular things. This system of using shapes to represent sounds was fast and efficient and spread quickly.

There are over 9000 languages in the world today and only 300 of them are written. Some writing systems use pictures to represent particular things, some use symbols to represent groups of sounds and others, like our alphabet, use a symbol to represent an isolated sound.

The alphabet we use developed gradually over thousands of years. Not all alphabets look like ours, and not all people write with the same tools. People wrote with many things throughout time–pointed sticks, hollow reeds, feathers and brushes.

Take a Look!

| Ancient Sumerian | Chinese Brush Writing | Ancient Greek | Russian Cryllic | Arabic |

The word *pen* comes from the Latin word *penna* which means "feather."

International Symbols

There are many alphabets and systems of writing around the world, but people have ways to communicate even when they do not share the same written or spoken language. How do you think people can communicate when they don't share the same written language?

A system of international symbols has been developed to help travelers at bus, train and air travel locations. These symbols make it easy for travelers to find their way even when they cannot speak or read a language.

Before viewing the following symbols, have students develop 10 symbols that they think would be important to the international community.

International Symbols

Lost & Found Left

Lockers Right

Elevators Downstairs

Food Downstairs

Arrivals Left

Departures Straight Ahead

Washrooms Straight Ahead

Taxi & Bus Stop Right

Road Signs
Simple symbols are used on roadways so travelers can view, understand and process information quickly. Have students re-create some common road signs or develop some new ones of their own.

Map Symbols
Maps use symbols to provide information and keep things simple. Take a look at a map. Record the symbols that you see. Make your own map and symbols.

Name _____

The Origins of Writing

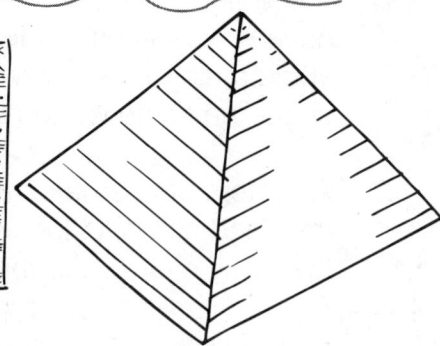

Draw a line to connect each word to its meaning.

pictogram   goat or sheep skin treated
                      so it can be written on

papyrus   a person who writes text by hand

parchment   Egyptian picture writing

petroglyphs   invented the printing press
                      in the 1450s

pulp   a specific mark used to
                      represent a sound in a
                      system of writing

scribe   a plant that can be made
                      into a form of writing paper

character   a soggy mass of wood or
                      other fiber that is used to
                      make paper

Johann Gutenberg   a picture symbol that
                      represents a word

hieroglyphics   a soft rock used to make
                      pencils

graphite   pictures and designs
                      painted or carved onto
                      rocks, caves or cliffs

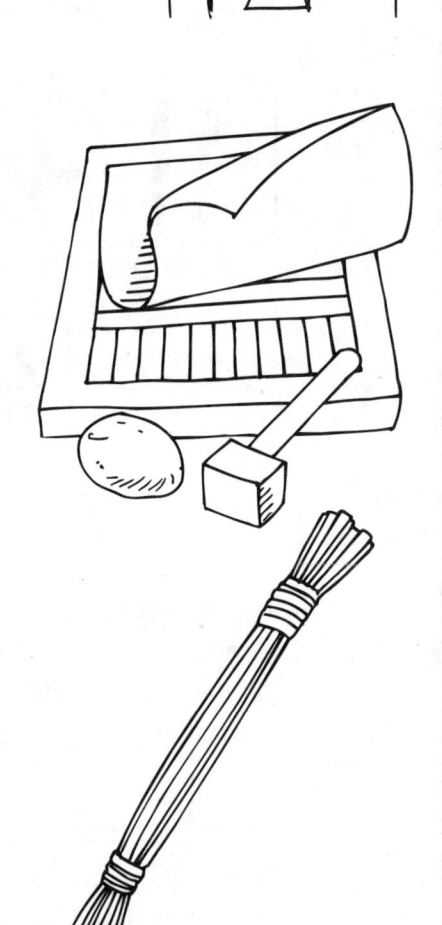

Chapter 2

For the Love of Language

Oral Language Experience

Oral language is a combination of effective listening and clear expression. It is a vital component of language development. Effective auditory discrimination and speech refinement are critical to a child's ability to make sense of print. Children who are competent oral communicators prove to be better writers.

Given the opportunities, children will use oral language to communicate needs, ideas, feelings and information as well as for play, song and the sheer joy of hearing the sound of their own voice!

Oral language can be experienced in one-on-one situations with peers, volunteers, school staff and educators, or in group settings with larger audiences in casual or formal settings. Provide many opportunities for children to observe, mimic, try out new sounds and words and give meaning to communications through oral expression.

The oral component of your language program should be central to all tasks. Oral language skills will translate into confidence and competence in all areas of language development. You may be surprised to find out that children in a safe learning environment won't just like to share their thoughts and written works . . . they will love it!

Oral Communication Skills Checklist

- ✓ listens to conversations, stories, discussions, films, songs, etc.
- ✓ listens for information
- ✓ listens to and follows several steps of directions
- ✓ communicates needs clearly through speech
- ✓ exhibits voice control
- ✓ uses language in a variety of ways
- ✓ demonstrates creativity in language usage
- ✓ exhibits confidence in oral expression
- ✓ expresses grade-appropriate ideas, opinions, feelings and thoughts
- ✓ makes use of a verbal vocabulary appropriate for grade level
- ✓ formulates questions to acquire information
- ✓ experiments with and enjoys language

Strategies to Get Young Writers Excited About Writing

The key to a successful writing program is a rich language environment that offers daily opportunities for reading, writing, speaking, listening and sharing ideas and written accomplishments.

✓ Make writing a positive experience that will help children to develop confidence in their new abilities.

✓ Provide developmentally appropriate activities that allow for personal development.

✓ Provide a space and activities which will encourage children to work independently or in the company of other children.

✓ Model enthusiasm for sounds, words, stories, books, resource information, your work and the work of others.

✓ Encourage sharing of ideas and works and dialogue about materials read or written by students or published authors.

✓ Host individual student-teacher writing conferences and assist children in compiling a writing portfolio.

✓ Provide formal instruction in the mechanics and conventions of writing to give children the tools they need to succeed! Follow up with activities, assistance and reviews of previously taught rules and skills.

✓ Reinforce concepts with active tasks that allow children to explore language in a variety of interesting ways.

✓ Provide daily access to free exploration of reading and writing centers and resources.

✓ Integrate assessment and teaching by providing immediate oral and written responses to work as often as possible, as well as assessment keys and a grading system with clear expectations.

Copycats

In this oral language activity, kids use their descriptive vocabulary skills to inspire reproductions of their own works of art.

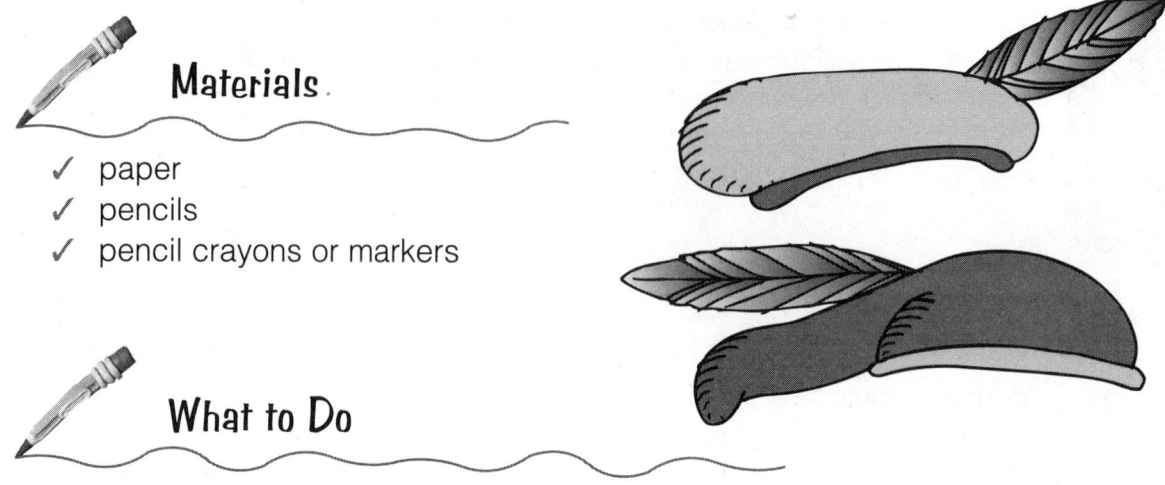

Materials

- ✓ paper
- ✓ pencils
- ✓ pencil crayons or markers

What to Do

1. Divide the children into pairs.
2. In each pair, one partner is the Master Artist and the other is the Reproduction Apprentice.
3. Have the Reproduction Apprentice turn away while the Master Artist goes to work drawing and then coloring a simple picture or geometric design on a blank piece of paper.
4. When the Master is finished, the Apprentice turns around to face her own piece of blank paper.
5. Holding the picture so that it is not visible to the Apprentice, the Master describes the picture, detail by detail. It is the job of the Apprentice to re-create the picture on her own piece of blank paper.
6. When the Apprentice is finished, place the two pieces of art side by side to determine how closely the reproduction resembles the original.
7. Display originals and reproductions, side by side, around the classroom or on a special bulletin board in the hall.

the Apprentice   the Master

Drawing

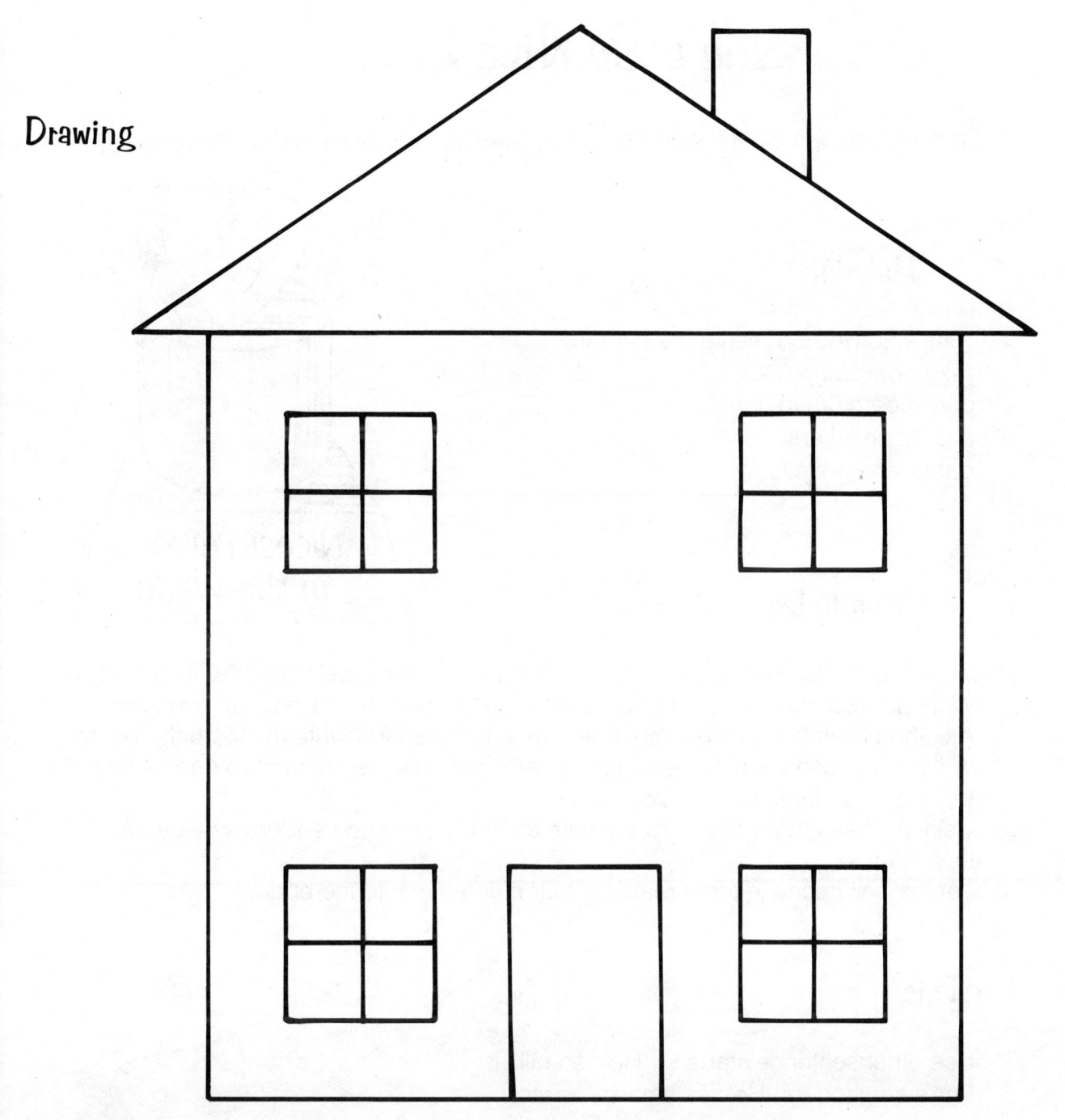

Description

This is a picture of a (turquoise) house. The house is a square, about 5" x 5" (13 x 13 cm), and it is situated in the middle of the page. The roof is a (red) triangle, about 2" (5 cm) high, the bottom edge of which overhangs the top of the house by about ½" (1.25 cm) on either side. There are four windows in the house and these are about 1" (2.5 cm) square each. Each is divided into four equal parts by two intersecting lines. Two windows are in the upper half of the house; two are in the lower half of the house. They are about ½" (1.25 cm) from the walls of the housetop, bottom and side to side. A (red) door, about 1½" (4 cm) tall and 1" (2.5 cm) wide, is positioned between the lower windows. Its top is parallel to their tops. A (yellow) chimney extends from the right side of the roof. It sits halfway along the triangle and rises up about 1" (2.5 cm) on the long side. The chimney top is parallel to the housetop.

She's So Nice . . .

Children use descriptive language and extravagance to explore personality.

Materials

- "She's So/He's So" sentence starters (examples on page 23)
- chalkboard or flip chart
- chalk or markers
- paper and pencils

Nicest Person in the World

What to Do

1. Write the "She's so nice . . ." sentence starter on the chalkboard (or flip chart).
2. Write a few of the sentence enders listed below on the board as an example.
3. Ask the children to call out other sentence enders, and write these on the board.
4. Write a new sentence starter on the board, and ask the children to copy it onto the top line of a blank piece of paper.
5. Using ellipses, have the children write as many sentence enders as they can on their pages.
6. Let the children take turns reading their different sentence enders.

Try This

- Use other sentence starters: He's so tall . . . She's so good . . . He's so smart . . ., etc.
- Use negative sentence starters: She's so mean . . . He's so angry . . . She's so out of it . . . He's so twisted . . . etc., but make sure the kids don't get out of hand. You might want to set some guidelines before starting.
- Hold a bragging contest. Have kids one-up each other. (I'm so strong . . . I can pick up a car with one hand. I'm so strong . . . I can throw a house, etc.)

Examples

She's so nice . . .

. . . she hasn't an enemy in the world.
. . . even a rabid dog wouldn't bite her.
. . . she gives her allowance to charity.
. . . she makes people happy just by being around.
. . . she lets everyone else have a turn first.
. . . she makes criminals want to go straight.
. . . she's almost too good to be true.
. . . she feeds every stray cat in the neighborhood.
. . . all the flowers nod their heads when she walks by.
. . . she makes people happy just by being around.
. . . she should win the Citizen of the Year Award.

The Angry Alphabet

In this takeoff on the traditional alliteration alphabet, kids learn that it is okay to demonstrate and vent anger with their words–and that it is possible to express hostility without the use of profanity.

Materials

✓ 27-page Angry Alphabet booklets (one for each child)
✓ pencils and crayons or markers

What to Do

1. Discuss *alliteration*–the stringing together of words that start with the same sound–and its use in the creation alphabet books for kids.
2. Introduce the Angry Alphabet as a more adventurous alternative targeted at older children.
3. Write the following "A" and "B" sentences on the board with lots of space for the insertion of angry adjectives:
    Aunt Angela ate an apple.
    Brother Bob bounces a ball.
4. Add adjectives with circles and lines until your sentences look like this:
    Angry, attacking ants ate Aunt Angela's acid apple.
    Bad brother Bob bounces a bowling ball in the bawling baby's buggy.
5. Have the children create their own Angry Alphabet in the blank booklet provided. Encourage the use of dictionaries and thesauri. This will help kids expand their sentences and their vocabularies!
6. Have the children illustrate their books.

Try This

✓ Have an Angry Alphabet Adulation lunch where kids get together, eat alphabet soup and admire one another's alphabet books.
✓ Create a "happy" alphabet. (Angelic Aunt Angela ate an amazing apple with absolute adulation.)

The "No-No" Game

In this letter elimination word game, children expand their vocabularies as they search for synonyms and develop questions and answers around imposed limitations.

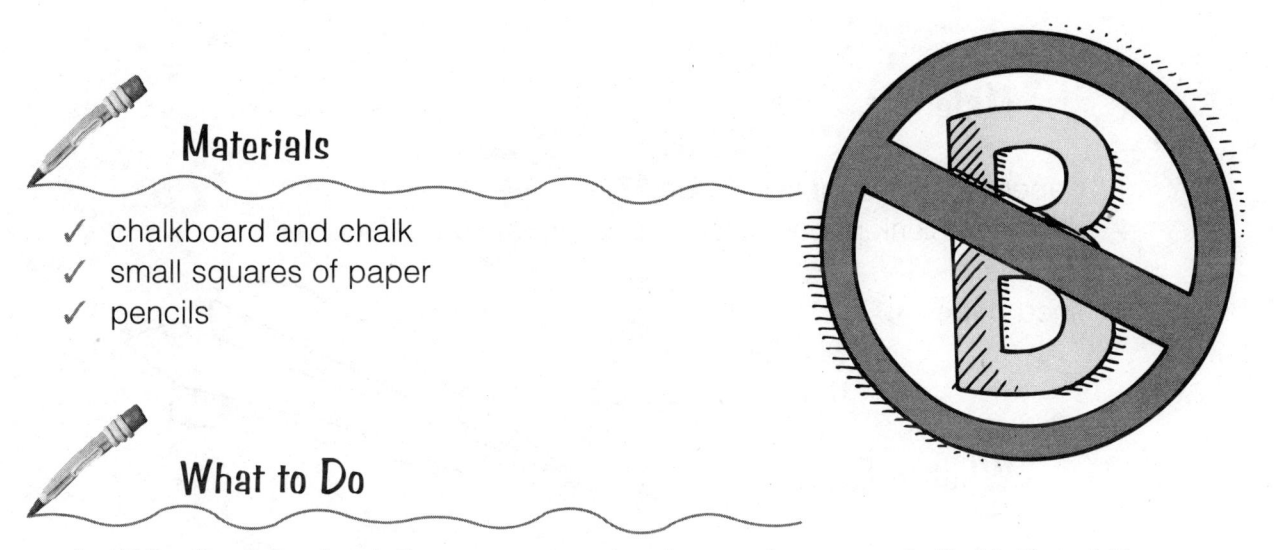

Materials

- chalkboard and chalk
- small squares of paper
- pencils

What to Do

1. Write the following letters on separate pieces of paper: *A, D, M, B* and *T*.
2. Place the pieces of paper facedown and mix.
3. Draw two. (The first letter applies to the asking part of the question-and-answer game, the second to the answering part.)
4. On the board, write a question with words that do not use the first letter.
5. Ask a student to answer the question using words that do not use the second letter. For example:

Where the "No-No" letters are	D–for the question T–for the answer
You might ask:	How can you tell time?
A student might answer:	Use a clock.

6. As a group, think of more questions and answers for these letters or draw two new "No-No" letters.
7. Have the children divide into pairs to play the game at their desks. Ask them to take turns asking and answering the questions. (Each pair will need one "No-No" letter set.)

Try This

- Simplify the game by substituting letters less commonly used in everyday language.
- Use two or more "No-No" letters per player.
- Establish a theme.
- Use "hard to avoid" letters. (G, M, O, I, S; S, A, N, T, I; or E, S, A, T, R)

Flights of Fancy

In this sentence starter activity that promotes fun, fitness and flight aerodynamics, paper airplanes give kids the inspiration they need to get writing!

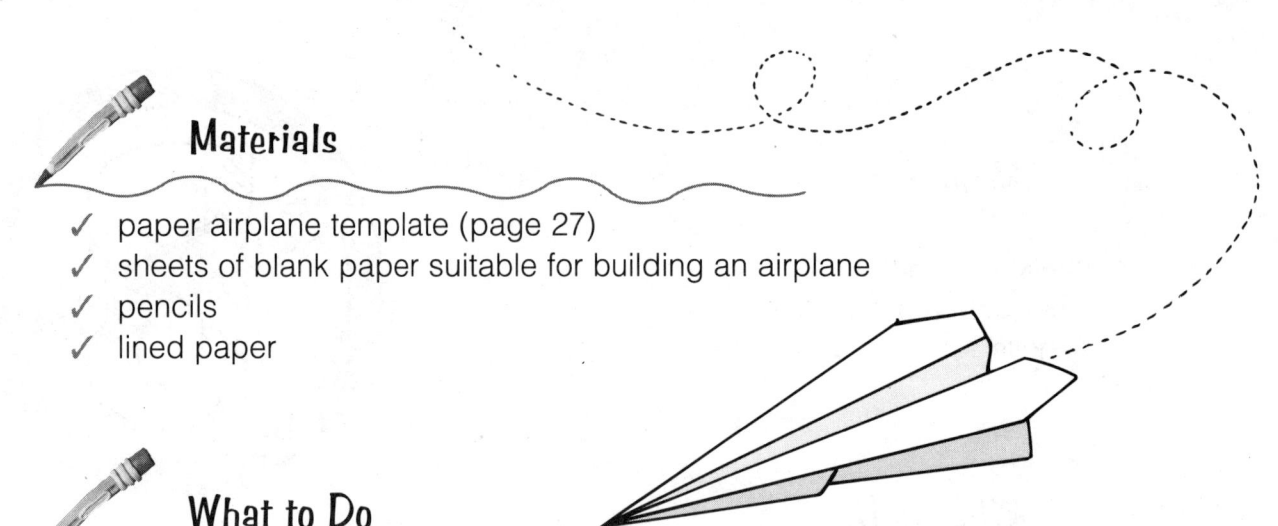

Materials

- ✓ paper airplane template (page 27)
- ✓ sheets of blank paper suitable for building an airplane
- ✓ pencils
- ✓ lined paper

What to Do

1. Hand one sheet of paper to each child.
2. Walk the children through a demonstration of "how to make a paper airplane."
3. Have each child write a word in pencil on one of the wings of his airplane.
4. Standing in a row at one end of the classroom, have the children launch their airplanes on a three-count.
5. After the airplanes have landed, ask the children to each retrieve one and return to their seats. (This is not a race. There are enough airplanes for everyone. There is no advantage to being the first person to a plane. In the event that a plane becomes lost, offer your plane as a substitute. If more than one plane gets lost, ask two children to share.)
6. Give the children two minutes to write a sentence using a word on their airplanes.
7. Line up and throw the planes again, repeating the exercise.

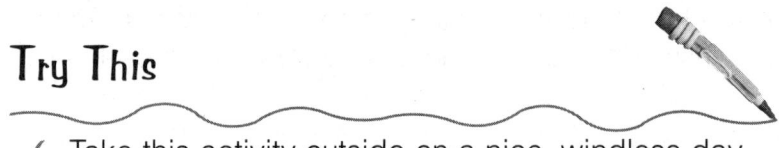

Try This

- ✓ Take this activity outside on a nice, windless day.
- ✓ Put a number of words on each plane. Have the children use them all in a single sentence or a short paragraph.

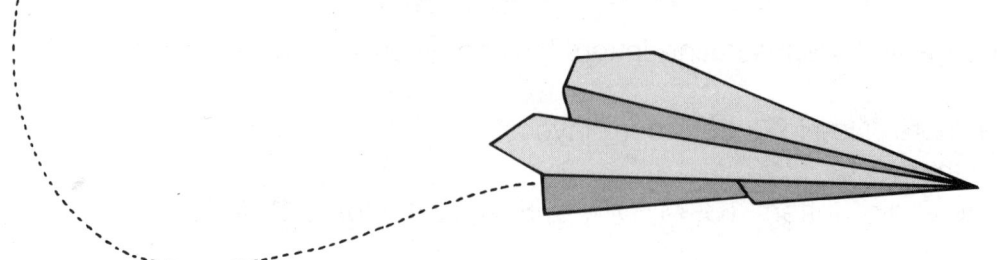

Flights of Fancy

Make a paper airplane!

What to Do

1. Fold a rectangular piece of paper vertically in half, and then open and make your paper flat again.

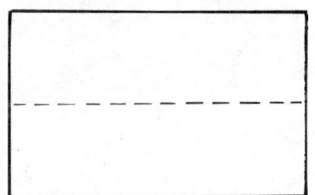

2. Fold the top corners down to meet the center fold line. This will form triangles in the top corners of the paper.

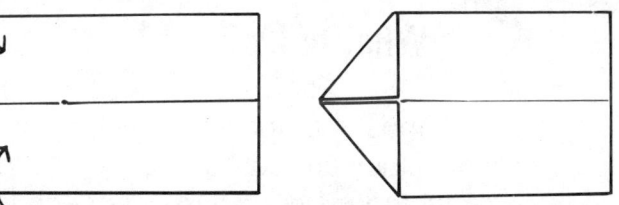

3. Fold the top corners down again to meet the center fold. Make a firm crease.

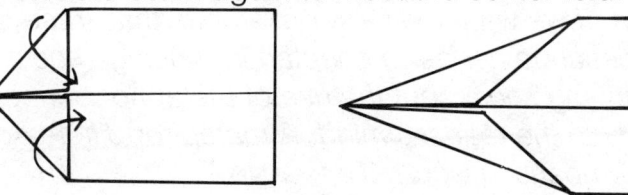

4. Fold the plane in half, folding it again on the pre-creased center fold.

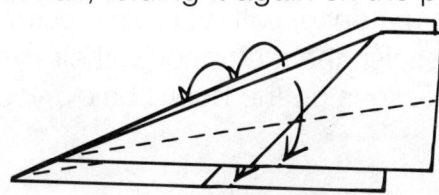

5. About 2" (5 cm) from the point that has formed, fold small wings out to the side.

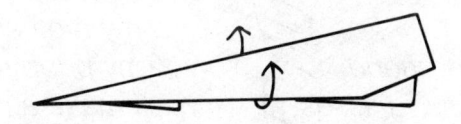

6. Hold the plane with the center fold at the bottom and fold the tips of the wings back out. Your plane is ready to fly!

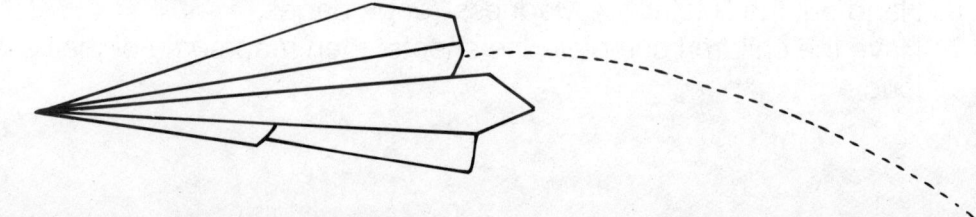

Metaphorically Speaking

In this copy page activity, children use metaphors to express and describe themselves.

Materials

- ✓ "Metaphor Madness" copy pages (pages 29-30)
- ✓ chalkboard or flip chart
- ✓ chalk or markers
- ✓ paper
- ✓ pencils

What to Do

1. Talk about metaphors: how they are used to enhance our writing and the way in which they are constructed.
   (A metaphor is a figure of speech that is used to liken one object to another by speaking of the object as if it were the other. We use metaphors to make our writing more vivid. If we want to say, for example, that Tracey is an incredibly fast runner, we can describe her as "a cheetah in running shoes." Tracey isn't really a cheetah in running shoes, but the use of metaphor brings a picture of speed and agility instantly to the reader's mind. A metaphor differs from a simile in that it does not use the comparison words **like** or **as**.)
2. Write the beginning of a metaphor on the board (or flip chart).
3. Using ellipses, finish the metaphor with your own comparison.
4. Then ask the children to finish the metaphor in their own words.
5. Write each of their suggestions on the board below yours.
   For example:

I am a black cloud when . . .
. . . I am angry at the world.
. . . I fail a test.
. . . I have a fight with my best friend.
. . . people tease me about my glasses.

I am a spring rain when . . .
. . . I get a present for no reason.
. . . my mother says she loves me.
. . . my puppy comes running to greet me.
. . . I make a new friend.

6. Hand out the "Metaphor Madness" copy pages.
7. Have the children complete the sheets; then read some of their metaphors out loud.

Name _____

Metaphor Madness

Show your true colors by finishing the following metaphorical sentences.

I am a ferocious lion when . . . _____

I am a gentle lamb when . . . _____

I am a cuddly bunny when . . . _____

I am a playful puppy when . . . _____

I am a strong bear when . . . _____

I am a proud peacock when . . . _____

I am a spinning spider when . . . _____

I am a nervous bird when . . . _____

I am a tough alley cat when . . . _____

I am a stubborn ox when . . . _____

I am a crowing rooster when . . . _____

I am a sly fox when . . . _____

I am a timid mouse when . . . _____

I am a creeping cockroach when . . . _____

I am a fish on a hook when . . . _____

I am a frightened fawn when . . . _____

I am a silly goose when . . . _____

Name _____

Metaphor Madness
continued

I am a nasty ogre when . . . _____

I am a sneaky spy when . . . _____

I am a super sleuth when . . . _____

I am a wicked witch when . . . _____

I am a quiet corner when . . . _____

I am a burning hot ember when . . . _____

I am a small, dark cave when . . . _____

I am an erupting volcano when . . . _____

I am an ice cold drink when . . . _____

I am a driving snowstorm when . . . _____

I am a dark and scary night when . . . _____

I am a cool and shady glen when . . . _____

I am a burbling brook when . . . _____

I am a raging river when . . . _____

I am a lonely beach when . . . _____

I am a peaceful forest when . . . _____

I am a bending blade of grass when . . . _____

Word Wizards

Create word magic when you make comparisons using the techniques outlined below.

A simile is a comparison made using *like* or *as*.
She pranced past like a saucy pony.
She was as pretty as a picture.

A metaphor makes a comparison without using *like* or *as*.
The sun was a golden balloon that floated above the clouds.

Personification gives a thing human qualities.
The sunflower kissed the bee.
The mother bear smiled to herself.

Materials

✓ shape cut-outs (bees, suns, flowers, raindrops, birds, baseballs, etc.)
✓ drawing and writing instruments

What to Do

1. Have students compare the cut-out object to something else using one of the techniques above. Focus on only one technique at a time.
2. Children will print the phrase on the shape and then draw and decorate the shape.
3. Attach a string and hang the word wonders from the ceiling or display on a theme bulletin board.

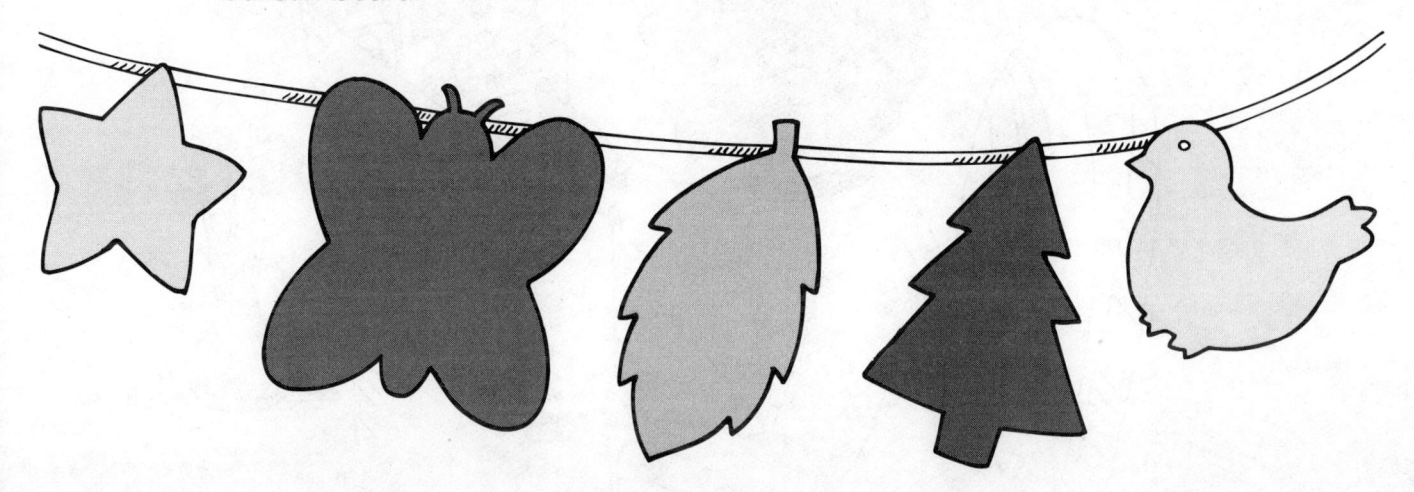

Synonym Sound-Alikes

Children use rhyme to find synonyms for cryptic clues.

Materials

- ✓ "Synonym Sound-Alikes" activity page, one for each child (page 33)
- ✓ paper
- ✓ pencils

What to Do

1. Give each child a copy of the "List Words" and the "Synonym Sound-Alikes" activity. *(Explain that **synonyms** are different words that express essentially the same idea.)*
2. For each "clue," ask the children to find a rhyming, two-word synonym. *(For example: "A super dish" could be a "great plate.")* One of each rhyming pair is a list word. To make things a little easier, the first letter of each rhyming pair is provided. *(The answers are on page 128.)*

Try This

- ✓ Have the children make up their own synonym sound-alikes and word list. Put these on a master list and photocopy. Repeat the exercise with this new copied page.

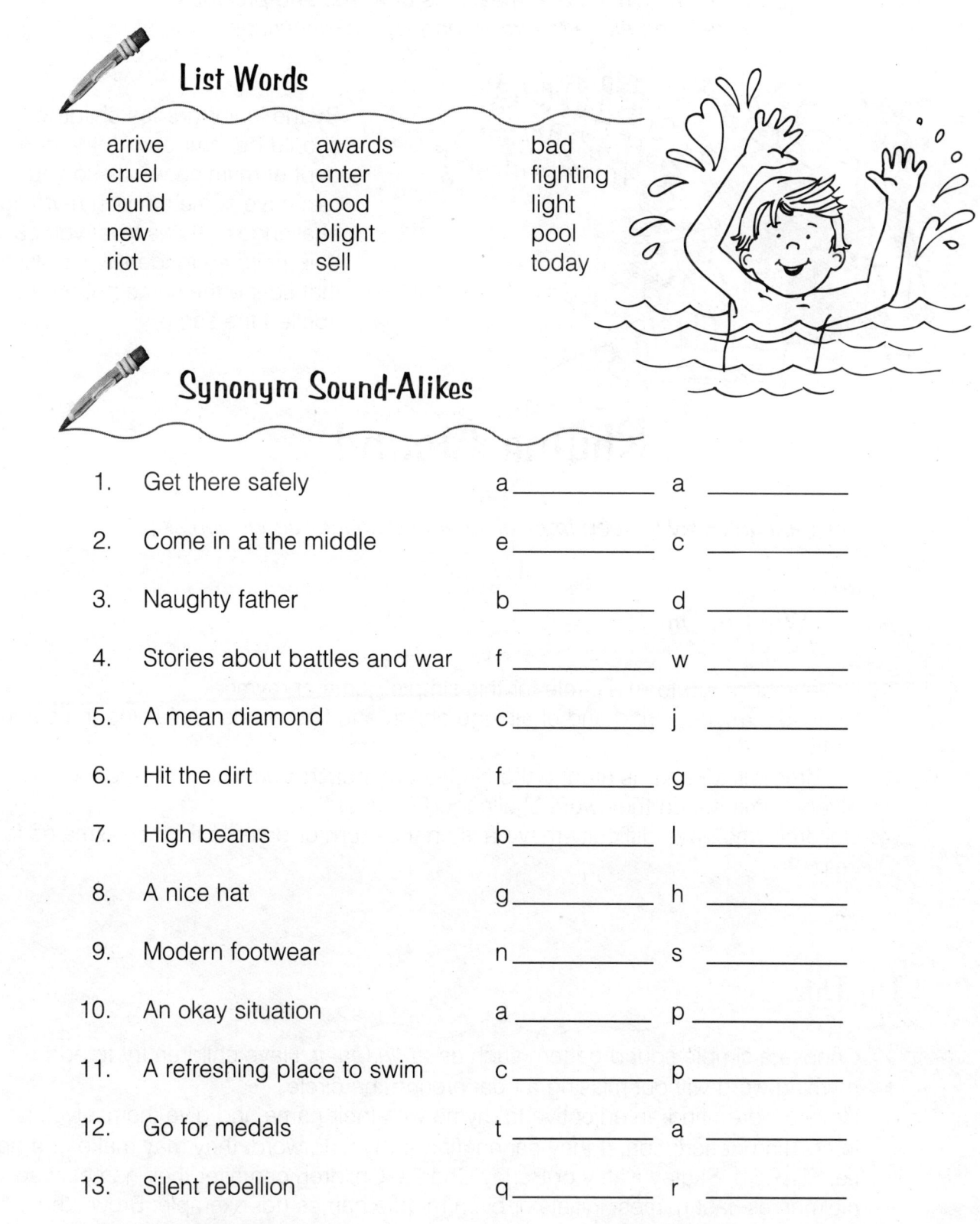

Name _____

Synonym Sound-Alikes

List Words

arrive	awards	bad
cruel	enter	fighting
found	hood	light
new	plight	pool
riot	sell	today

Synonym Sound-Alikes

1. Get there safely — a_____ a_____
2. Come in at the middle — e_____ c_____
3. Naughty father — b_____ d_____
4. Stories about battles and war — f_____ w_____
5. A mean diamond — c_____ j_____
6. Hit the dirt — f_____ g_____
7. High beams — b_____ l_____
8. A nice hat — g_____ h_____
9. Modern footwear — n_____ s_____
10. An okay situation — a_____ p_____
11. A refreshing place to swim — c_____ p_____
12. Go for medals — t_____ a_____
13. Silent rebellion — q_____ r_____
14. Marketing success — s_____ w_____
15. Have fun now — p_____ t_____

Poetry Primer

Poetry sets the stage for exciting word play. Its opens children's ears and hearts to the wonderful sounds and meanings of words and provides a stepping-stone to further language experiences.

By the junior grades children should be familiar with the concept of rhyming words so you can have some fun with rhyming challenges. At this level you can help children to identify words that sound the same but are not spelled the same.

Rhyme Around

A kid-friendly way to keep track of letter and sound recognition skills!

What to Do

1. Have your group form a circle for this simple game of rhyme.
2. Choose a rhyme sound and challenge children to find words containing the same sound.
3. Children will take turns around the circle contributing a word that rhymes with the given rhyme sound they were challenged to meet.
4. Children who have difficulty may pass on their turn or defer to their classmates for help.

Try This

- ✓ Choose a simple sound pattern such as *at, in, an, it*. Have children try to add a rhyming word without missing a beat around the circle.
- ✓ Have children find an adjective to rhyme with their name and give themselves an interesting description. If they cannot find a rhyming word, they may make one up, i.e. Slim Jim, Skatey Katey or Barley Charlie. Children can alter their names, use nicknames, last names, initials or even middle names (for example: Brown the Clown, Meg the Egg).

What Is a Poem?

A poem is a collection of words that are placed creatively to capture a feeling, project an image or express an idea. Poems tell stories–in a few words or a few pages.

Although some poetry is written in free verse, poetry writing often follows a pattern of rhythm or rhyme. Poems have a special look, a special sound and a special way of getting ideas across. In a poem, the flow of words is very important, so listen carefully!

Share a Poem

Share a poem using an experience chart, overhead or other visual aid. Have children listen for the rhyming words and help to mark these on your visual aid. Talk about the sounds, look and flow of the words. What did children notice about the reading? Compare different poetry forms. Have children memorize and recite a poem. This experience invites children into the oral language experience of a poem.

Fun with Free Verse

Free verse poetry is a fun starting place for young poetry writers. It gives novice poets the freedom to decide the length of the poem, whether or not it will rhyme and how it will look.

What to Do

1. Pick a subject.
2. Brainstorm to collect ideas about your subject.
3. Cross out your least interesting ideas, and work with your best!
4. Put your ideas together in an interesting, creative way.
5. Read and revise your poem.
6. Edit and proofread.
7. Make a final copy ready for publication.

Kid Stuff

crayons, marbles, running shoes
skis and skates and roller blades
muddy handprints on the wall
rubber boot prints down the hall
storybooks and hopscotch chalk
puppy dogs and scruffy cats
giggles in the dark

Couplet Capers

In this poetry activity, children use a two-line rhyme to express a thought.

Materials

✓ paper
✓ pencils

What to Do

1. Have the children write a rhyming couplet: a two-line rhyming verse that expresses a single thought:
   Back and forth the lion stalked.
   Prowling, growling as he walked.
   or   Cheevy! Cheevy! chirped the bird
           Greeting all with this one word.
   or   Steven sat upon the chair
           And fixed me with an angry stare.
2. See if the children can tell a short story using four rhyming couplets.
   1) The other day, when I was bad,
      The teacher phoned and told my dad.
   2) When I came home he bade me in
      And took me firmly by the chin.
   3) What's this I hear?" he said to me.
      "Did teacher catch you in the tree?"
   4) "Oh, no," said I, "Dad, not at all"
      "She caught me so's to break my fall!"

Try a four-line story in which each couplet uses the same rhyme.
   1) Last Friday morn when I awoke
      No words came out when first I spoke.
   2) I hemmed and hawed and gave a choke,
      And then I heard a froggy croak.
(Add on, if possible)
   3) I squeezed my throat and gave a poke,
      But he stuck fast, the rotten bloke.
   4) He seemed to laugh as my voice broke,
      But I did not enjoy the joke.

Haiku

Framing a haiku poem will help children develop an ear for syllable counts and symmetry as they carefully choose words that convey tone, meaning or thought.

Haiku (hi-ku) is a traditional Japanese form of poetry that focuses on nature. This three-line poem follows a specific syllable pattern.

Line 1:	5 syllables	*Little snowflakes fell,*
Line 2:	7 syllables	*like tiny crystal dancers*
Line 3:	5 syllables	*waiting for a thaw.*

What to Do

1. Choose a subject. (It is not necessary to focus on nature.)
2. Observe or let your imagination take over.
3. Write your ideas.
4. Pull your poem together.
5. Count your syllables.
6. Revise if necessary.
7. Edit and proofread.
8. Complete a final copy.

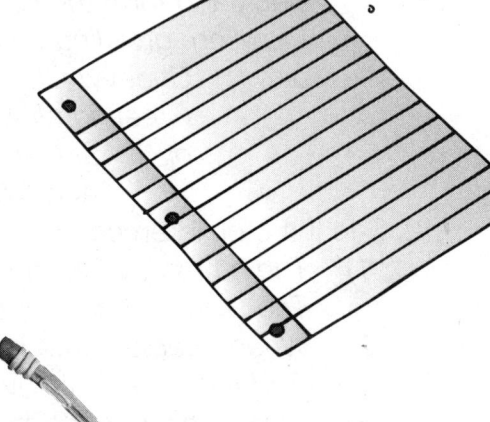

Try This

✓ Display your haiku poetry on a bulletin board for all to enjoy. Cut a green and brown bonsai tree from construction paper. Paste poems in the leafy bulges of the tree. Staple the tree to a stark blue background.

Plain Cinquain

*In writing a structured cinquain poem,
children learn to describe a subject–and the way they feel about it.*

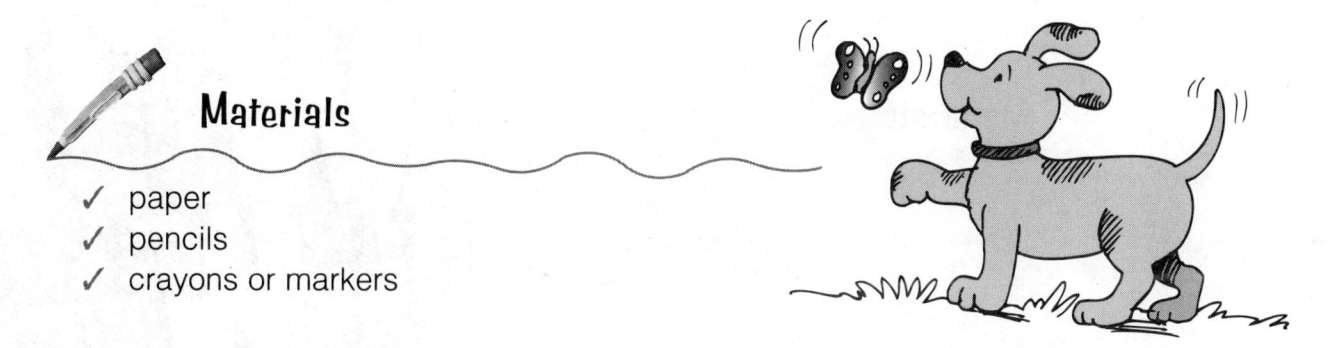

Materials

- paper
- pencils
- crayons or markers

What to Do

1. Have the children write a cinquain, using the following formula:
   Line 1: one word, a subject or an idea
   Line 2: two words, adjectives describing the subject
   Line 3: three words, verbs related to the subject
   Line 4: four words, telling your reaction to the subject
   Line 5: one word, a synonym for the subject

Dog
Loyal, affectionate
Running, jumping, playing
My very best friend
Buster

Try This

- Have the students think up a crazy name for a monster or an alien and describe their creation in a cinquain. Ask them to draw it.
- Have the students write two cinquains about themselves: one showing their good side, one showing their rotten side.
- Get emotional. Have the kids write a cinquain about an emotion.

The Five Ws Poem

*Children learn how to use the five Ws to tell a short story
in this fun and easy poetry writing exercise.*

Materials

- paper
- pencils

What to Do

1. Have the children write a five-line pyramid poem in which each line answers one of the "Five Ws": who, what, where, when and why?
   (who)   Tracey
   (what)   Likes to write
   (where)   At her computer
   (when)   In the middle of the night
   (why)   Because her mind is wide awake.
2. The poems can be organized in one of three ways: flushed left (above), centered (below) or flushed right (below right).

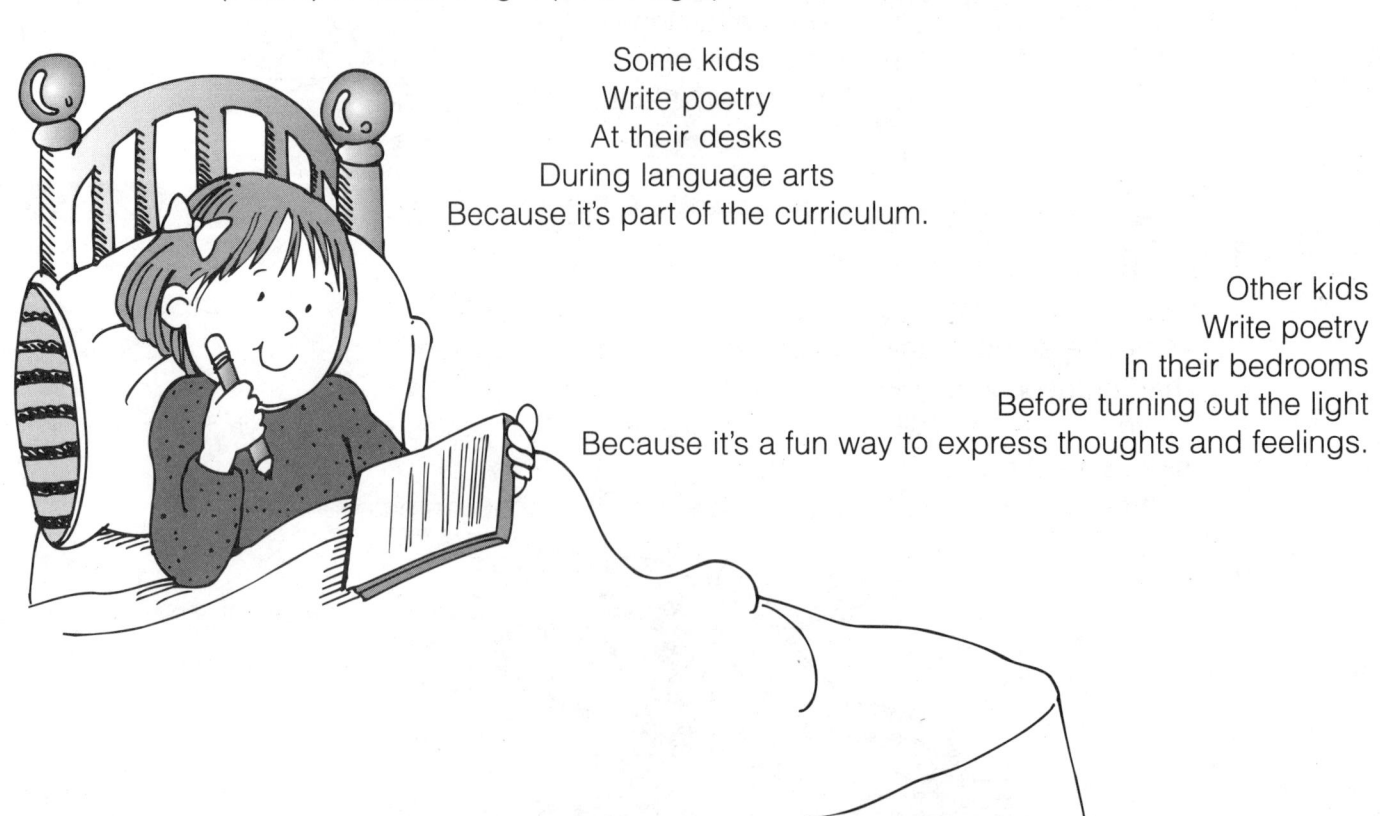

Some kids
Write poetry
At their desks
During language arts
Because it's part of the curriculum.

Other kids
Write poetry
In their bedrooms
Before turning out the light
Because it's a fun way to express thoughts and feelings.

Chapter 3

The Right Stuff

Let's Write!

Your Writing Folder
Every student should have a writing folder with a storage pocket for works in progress. Original drafts should be valued and kept. Emphasize that these drafts are masterpieces, because this is the point where their thoughts first met the paper.

Writing Portfolio
Students should have a writing portfolio to collect samples of edited and unedited work throughout the year. Teachers and students should be involved in deciding which works should be included.

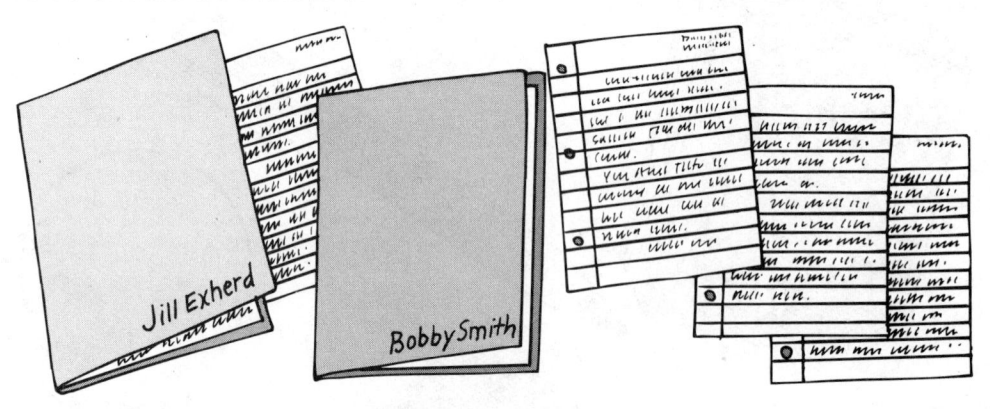

Getting Started

Sometimes getting started is the hardest part of writing a story! New writers often need a little help to get going or to take their writing in a new direction.

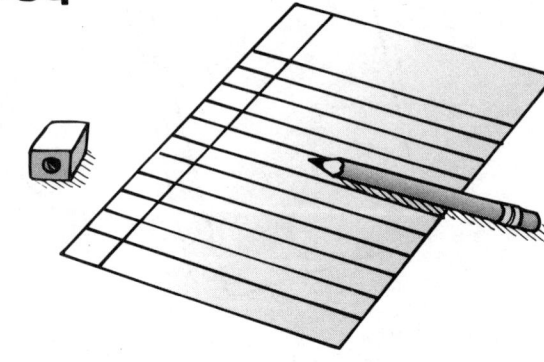

Ideas to Get You Started

✓ Write about something that crosses your path today.
✓ Look at something old in a new way.
✓ Use material from a school project to set the scene for a story.
✓ Let your knowledge of a particular subject lead the way.
✓ Find inspiration in your favorite books.
✓ Turn to your interests and hobbies for material from real-life situations.
✓ Open your mind and let your imagination run wild. You might discover characters, scenes and stories that you never knew you knew!

Timed Writing

Bring pencils and paper to the creative process every day. Practice makes perfect! Writers who practice their newfound skills daily will find their talent improves exponentially.

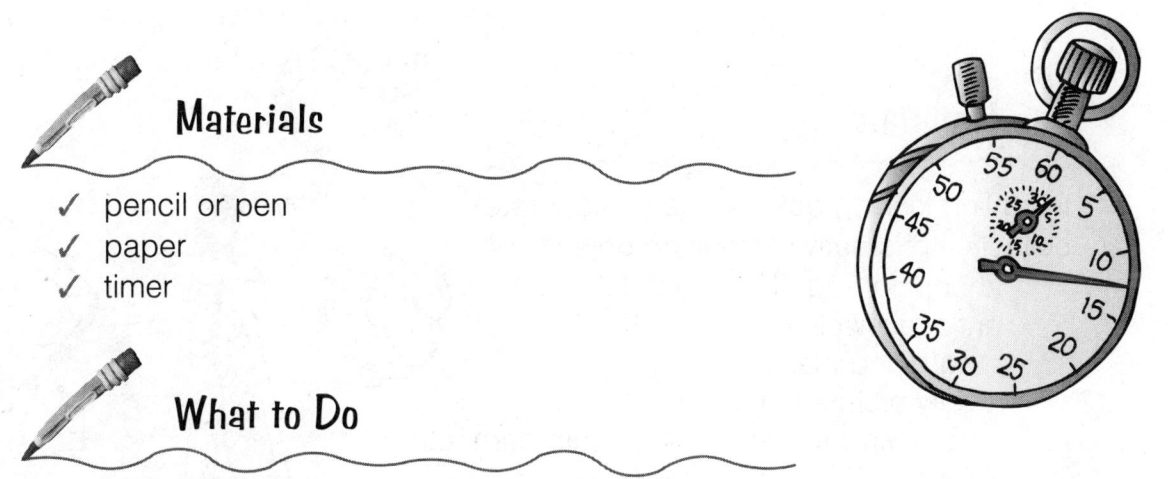

Materials

- ✓ pencil or pen
- ✓ paper
- ✓ timer

What to Do

1. Explain to students that this writing exercise will help them practice their skills and put their ideas on paper.
2. Have students write for a designated time period. Start by setting a timer for two minutes. Work up to five and then 10 minutes.
3. The idea is for young writers to keep their pens moving the entire time. Stopping is not allowed. They are to write whatever comes into their heads without concern for grammar or spelling. Let the stream of consciousness flow and the pencils go. This exercise gets easier with practice.
4. When time is up, have students put down their pencils, no matter how enthusiastic they are to keep going. (The kids can pick up these ideas later and continue.)
5. Encourage students to share their work. Sometimes the work is brilliant, sometimes it is silly, but it is always good practice.

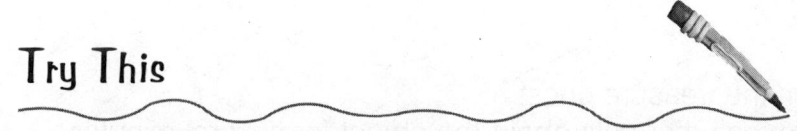

Try This

- ✓ You can inspire writers by providing topics for timed writings. Supply a noun, verb, adjective or adverb; open a dictionary page and point to any word; hand out fortune cookies or pull something out of the "Treasure Chest" (page 44) for inspiration.

Hold That Thought!

When a great thought comes, don't let it get away. Jot down some key words that will help you to "hold that thought."

Treasure Chest

*Children put their imaginations to work
as they delve into this treasure trove of inspirational gems.*

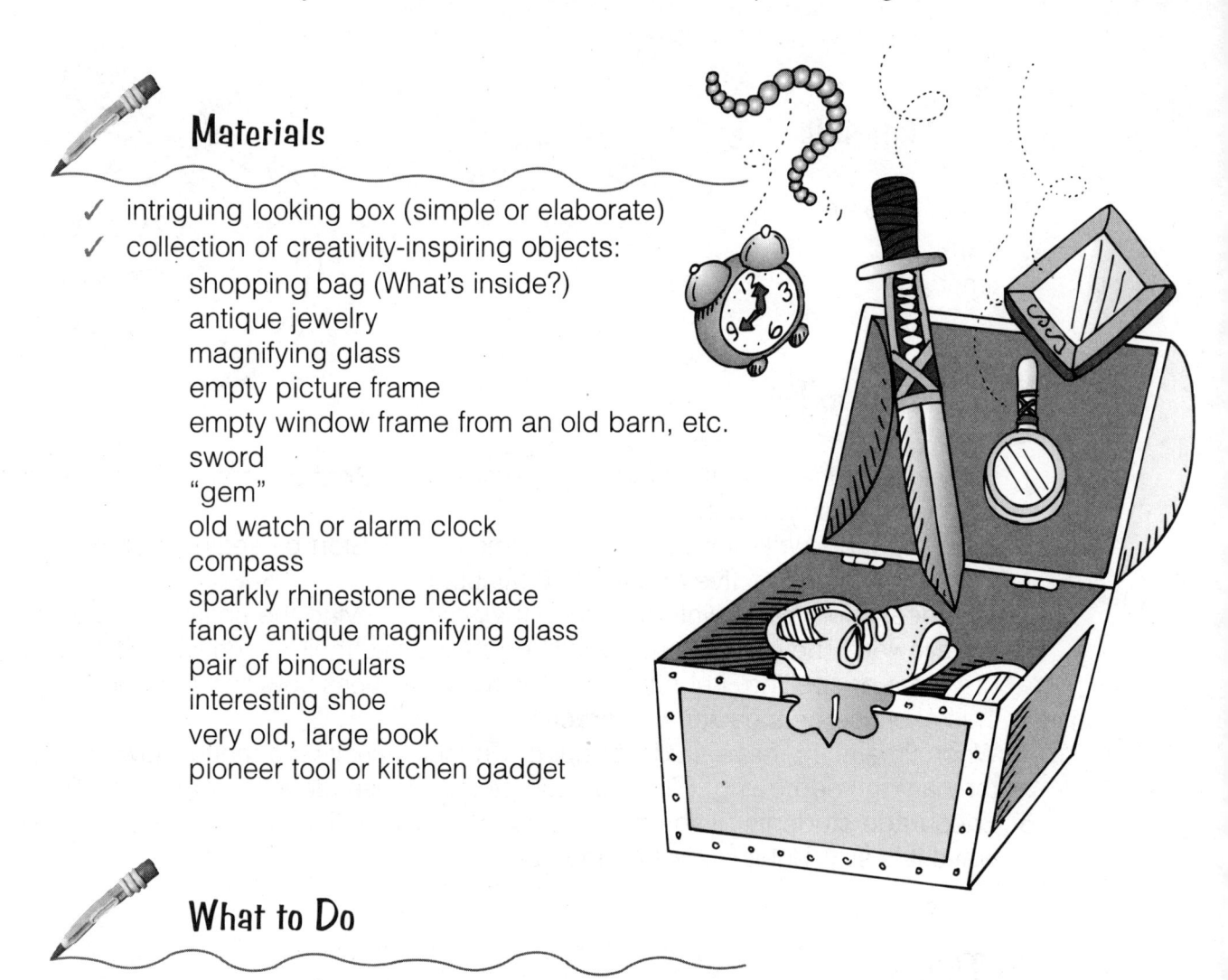

Materials

- intriguing looking box (simple or elaborate)
- collection of creativity-inspiring objects:
    - shopping bag (What's inside?)
    - antique jewelry
    - magnifying glass
    - empty picture frame
    - empty window frame from an old barn, etc.
    - sword
    - "gem"
    - old watch or alarm clock
    - compass
    - sparkly rhinestone necklace
    - fancy antique magnifying glass
    - pair of binoculars
    - interesting shoe
    - very old, large book
    - pioneer tool or kitchen gadget

What to Do

1. Pick an object from the treasure chest.
2. Have children write their thoughts about the object for several minutes.
3. Have students share their writings about the object.
4. As an alternative, ask questions about the object and have children write their answers.
5. Share these thoughts.

Inspiring Questions

Where did this item come from? Who owns or once owned it?
What is it? What is it used for? Who is looking for this object?
Why is it so important to its owner?

Unlock Your Imagination

Find the key that unlocks your imagination.

Capture your creativity.

Believe that anything is possible.

Stretch your imagination.

Don't be shy.

Listen to your heart.

See what is not there and then imagine it is.

Time travel . . .

Write to the music.

Escape.

What if . . .

Write what's on your mind.

Transform anything into anything.

Daydream.

SAY IT YOUR OWN WAY.

Close your eyes and imagine . . .

Don't Miss a Thing

Good writers don't let anything escape their scrutiny.

Materials

- ✓ large serving tray
- ✓ 20 assorted items (i.e. spoon, scissors, egg cup, shoelace, coin, paper clip)
- ✓ towel or cloth large enough to cover the tray and items
- ✓ timer

What to Do

Activity 1
1. Present the tray full of items for children to view for one minute.
2. Cover the tray with the towel.
3. Ask students to recall the 20 items on the tray.

Activity 2
1. Display the objects for all to see.
2. Choose one or more keen observers to leave the room. While these students are out of the room, have another child remove an item from the tray.
3. Invite the students to return. Can they tell you which item was taken away?

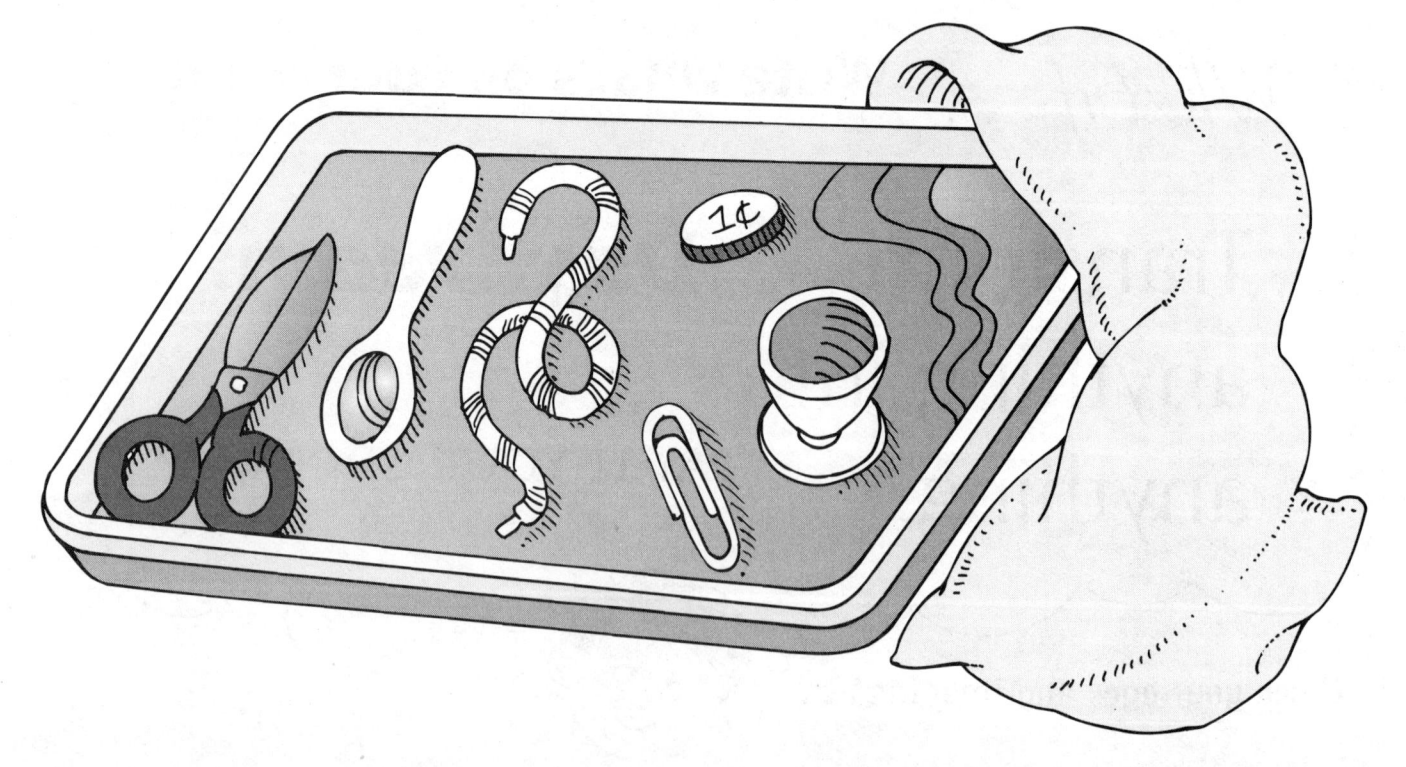

Silly Sentences

In this hilarious game that introduces kids to the five Ws, promotes creative thinking; encourages reading; and helps to teach sentence structure, sequencing and numbering concepts, kids learn that all writing is good writing–especially when it's silly!

Materials

- ✓ tagboard, divided into Silly Sentence Grid (page 49)
- ✓ marker
- ✓ two dice
- ✓ five place markers
- ✓ Silly Sentences Flip-Up Books (page 48)

Get Ready

1. Turn the tagboard vertically so that it is taller than it is wide.
2. Make four vertical lines down the length of the board, dividing it into five columns.
3. Divide the board into 60 boxes by drawing 12 evenly spaced horizontal lines across it.
4. In the boxes along the top row, print the following headings: *WHO? DID WHAT? WHERE? WHEN?* and *WHY?*
5. In the first left-hand column, print the numbers from one (1) to twelve (12), leaving the top box empty.
6. Your grid is now ready to be mounted on a vertical surface.

Who?	Did What?	Where?	When?	Why?
1.				
2.				
3.				
4.				
5.				
6.				
7.				
8.				
9.				
10.				
11.				
12.				

How to Play

1. Have the children provide you with enough "WHO?s", "DID WHAT?s", "WHERE?s", "WHEN?s" and "WHY?s" to fill the grid. (See the Silly Sentences Sample Grid on page 49.) Stick to one gender and use only the pronoun he/his or she/her. Using the two interchangeably does not work. (*My, I,* and *our* and *we* are fine to use.)
2. After the grid is complete, have the children take turns rolling the two dice. After the first roll, ask the child to determine the sum of the dice and place a marker on the "WHO?" space that corresponds to that sum in the number column. Ask different children to do the same for the second, third, fourth and fifth rolls, placing a marker on the "DID WHAT?" "WHERE?" "WHEN?" and "WHY?" spaces.
3. When each column has a marker in it, choose a child to read aloud the silly sentence.
4. When the laughter has subsided–this game is guaranteed to cause hysterics –remove the markers and begin a new round.

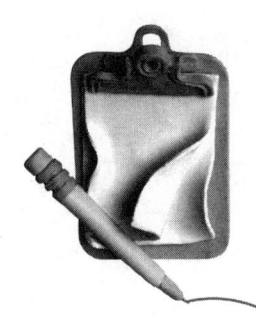

Silly Sentences Flip-Up Book

✓ To make a Silly Sentences Flip-Up Book, copy the Silly Sentences Grid onto an 8½" x 11" (22 x 28 cm) sheet of paper, omitting the numbers 1-12.
✓ Photocopy the grid so that you have one sheet for every child.
✓ Cut the grid across the rows so that you have 13 vertical strips of paper. (The *WHO? DID WHAT? WHERE? WHEN? WHY?* strip will be the cover page.)
✓ Assemble the Silly Sentences Flip-Up Book by layering the 13 strips on top of one another in any order. (The cover strip must be on top.)
✓ Attach the strips by stapling horizontally across the top.
✓ Make vertical cuts in the strips between the *WHO? DID WHAT? WHERE? WHEN? WHY?* columns. Be sure not to cut all the way to the top.
✓ To make a silly sentence, flip up a different number of pages in each column.

Silly Sentences Sample Grid

	Who?	Did What?	Where?	When?	Why?
1.	The king	spilled water	on the throne	while he was talking	because he was distracted.
2.	My dad	dropped a jar	on the floor	in the garage	because his hands were slippery.
3.	Susan's dog	buried the bone	in our garden	last summer	because he felt like it.
4.	The supervisor	gave a detention	in the yard	at recess	as punishment.
5.	Our preacher	said a special prayer	in church	on Sunday	around Christmastime.
6.	The T-Rex	killed a raptor	in the Jurassic Period	65 million years ago	because he was hungry.
7.	The principal	started yelling	over the P.A. system	in his office	because he was angry.
8.	The teacher	read a story	in circle	before snack time	as a reward.
9.	My pet lizard	ate a mouse	in the terrarium	at night	while we were sleeping.
10.	A police officer	arrested a bad guy	in an aisle	at the store	during a robbery.
11.	My doctor	took my temperature	in my mouth	when I was sick	because he had to.
12.	A horse	bucked a cowboy	into the dirt	at the rodeo	during a stampede.

49

TLC10203 Copyright © Teaching & Learning Company, Carthage, IL 62321-0010

Playing with Paragraphs

In this activity, kids learn about paragraphs and how to construct the four paragraph types.

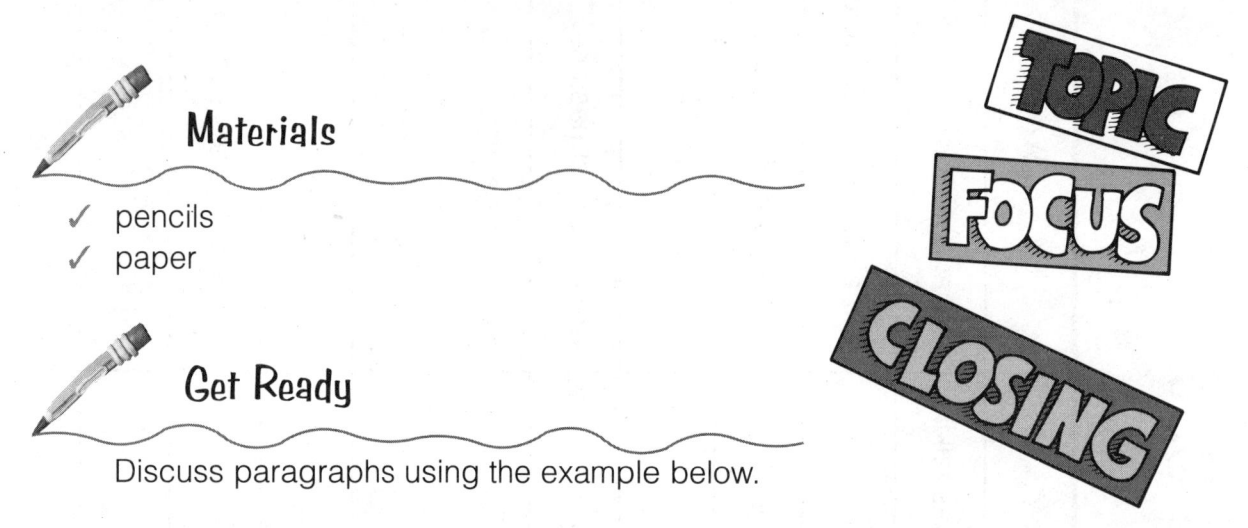

Materials

- pencils
- paper

Get Ready

Discuss paragraphs using the example below.

(There are three parts to every paragraph, the topic sentence, the body and the closing sentence. The topic sentence tells the reader what the paragraph is about by introducing a subject and a focus. The body of the paragraph includes a number of sentences that give the reader all the information required to understand the topic. The closing sentence sums up the information or tells what the information means.)

On Monday, our class (*topic*) went to the zoo (*focus*). We learned all about endangered species from our guide, Harry. He took us to see many animals that are extremely rare–or even nonexistent–in the wild. He told us how human beings are destroying the animals' habitat to build houses and harvest lumber. It was sad to see all those beautiful creatures behind bars, but Harry said that for some animals, zoos are their last chance for survival. He explained that zoos around the world are cooperating to breed animals in captivity in the hopes that one day they can be returned to their native homes (*body*). The zoo is a wonderful place, not only for the people who visit, but also for the lucky animals that call it home . . . for now (*closing sentence*).

There are four types of paragraphs:

I. Descriptive paragraph: describes a person, place or thing using the senses.

II. Narrative paragraph: tells a story by sharing the details of an experience.

III. Persuasive paragraph: gives the writer's opinion on a topic and tries to convince the reader that this is the right opinion.

IV. Expository paragraph: gives information about a topic (explains ideas, gives directions or shows how to do something using transition words such as *first*, *second* and *third*).

What to Do

1. Have the children write a paragraph. Don't worry about paragraph type. Just make sure the paragraph has a topic sentence, a body and a closing sentence.
2. Share some of the paragraphs out loud. Identify the topic sentence, the body and the closing sentence.
3. When they are comfortable with paragraph structure, have the children write and share one paragraph of each type, using the examples on page 52.

Descriptive

Our corner bakery is the most delicious place on Earth. As soon as you walk in the door, the hot, sweet smell of fresh-baked bread assaults your nostrils. Soft, fluffy buns –still steaming–fill the counter to overflowing in a row of brown woven baskets. Behind two glass panels sit treats of the most scrumptious kind: chocolate eclairs, bulging with cream; butter tarts oozing with raisin syrup; cupcakes piled high with brightly colored jelly beans; and cookies that are more chocolate chunk than cookie. To stroll the aisles of our corner bakery is to walk the paths of heaven.

Narrative

The other day, my dog Samuel just about got himself killed. We were visiting with his Beagle friend, Little Jimminy, from down the street. The three of us were having a grand old stroll along the back alley looking for treasure. Suddenly Samuel caught sight of a squirrel in a garbage can. Now, Samuel's not a big dog–he's a Jack Russell Terrier–but he sure can jump. He lit off after that squirrel and leapt right over Old Man Frosty's back fence. Well, Frosty doesn't cotton to dogs. Before you could say "yee haw," I heard a shot and Samuel came skittering back over the fence, a spray of buckshot poking out of his hind quarters. My goodness, but Doc Harlowe did have a go at that poor dog's back end. Looking at those stitches, I don't reckon Sammy will be jumping fences for a while!

Persuasive

Jennifer is a very kind person. She is always doing things for other people: walking their dogs, helping them with their homework, giving them bits of her lunch, taking the blame for their mistakes. When she is not helping out her classmates, she is volunteering at the local long-term care facility: listening to people talk, helping them with crafts, ghostwriting notes to their friends and family. She never seems to take a minute to think about herself and her own needs. She is a perfect role model. I think Jennifer should be nominated for Citizen of the Year.

Expository

If you are camping in the wilderness, make sure you take precautions to discourage nocturnal visitors. First, keep your food in airtight containers and store them in your car. Second, string your garbage from a tree. Third, pitch your tent close to your vehicle. Fourth, and finally, carry a cellular phone with you at all times. If you ever find yourself separated from a thousand pound black bear by a 1/8" (.3 cm) piece of car window glass, I think you'll find it comes in pretty handy!

Brainstorming

*In this cooperative thinking activity,
children "piggyback" their imaginations to generate a list of related ideas.*

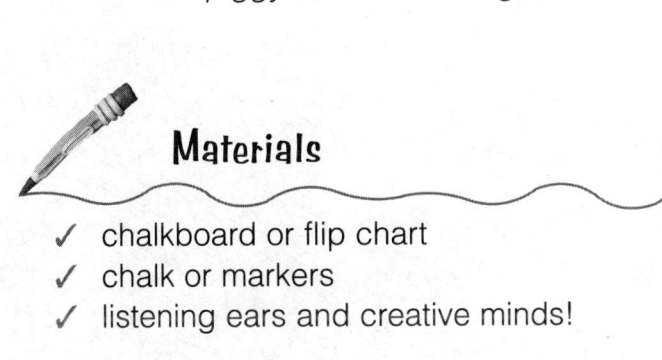

Materials

- ✓ chalkboard or flip chart
- ✓ chalk or markers
- ✓ listening ears and creative minds!

What to Do

1. Have the children sit in a group on the floor.
2. Ask one child to name a person, place or thing. (You might want to choose a noun related to a relevant or timely classroom theme.)
3. Write this word on the board (or chart). It is now the "theme" for your brainstorming activity.
4. Ask the children to call out different ideas relating to your theme.
5. Write each of these on the board or chart. (Beach-related words and thoughts might include: *sand, sand castles, shovels, pails, burying my dad, hot, summer, vacation, sunscreen, hat, suntan, water, waves, children, laughing, running, swimming, splashing, diving, lots of fun, bathing suit, towel, beach umbrella, shady, picnic lunch*, etc.)
6. Keep going until the ideas are exhausted. (Emphasize that there are no "rights" and "wrongs" in this exercise. The purpose of brainstorming is to generate innovative ideas and solutions by stimulating and unleashing the unique creative genius that exists within every human being.)

Try This

- ✓ As a group, develop a poem using the words on the board. (You can add words to improve the flow or imagery of your poem.)

  The Beach
  Summer vacation, summer fun and a sunny, summer trip to the beach. Laughing children, sunscreened and suntanned, run–hats flying–across the hot sand and disappear beneath the waves. Swimming, splashing, they break from the water and stagger back to beach towels, beach umbrellas and a shady picnic lunch. Stomachs full, they turn to sand pails, sand shovels, sand castles and Dad, buried alive. Too soon, they trudge back to a blistering car–wet feet crunching in sandy shoes–sad, but satisfied; tired, but happy.

- ✓ Don't use a theme. Just throw out a thought and develop a list of ideas word association style.

Clustering

In this activity, children learn how to "cluster" their thoughts around a central conflict to develop the beginning, middle and end of a story.

Materials

✓ chalkboard or flip chart
✓ chalk or markers

What to Do

1. Discuss the object of clustering: organized brainstorming that "clusters" thoughts around, or builds outwards from, a single, central thought.
2. Draw a tree trunk in the middle of the chalkboard or chart.
3. Write a one-sentence scenario in the trunk. This central idea will be the conflict. (I lost my running shoes; My dog ran away; I had a fight with my best friend; I have to sing a solo at our school concert; etc.)
4. Working backward, ask the children to think about what might have happened to cause the problem.
5. Put each of these ideas in a root growing down from the tree. (Each of these roots represents a possible story beginning.)
6. Then refer back to the problem and ask the children about the possible implications of the problem, in other words, what might happen next. (The conflict and resolution are the real "meat" or middle of a story.)
7. Put each idea in a branch growing from the trunk of the tree.
8. For each implication, ask the children to think about a potential resolution (ending) to the story that is taking shape. Print each idea in a leaf.
9. Show children how each root/trunk/branch/leaf idea can be used as the beginning, middle and end of a story.
10. Write a story using one of the complete scenarios.

Try This

✓ Add more detail conflict or resolution detail by drawing a twig from each branch before adding the leaves.
✓ Another cluster concept:
   - Sandwich Clusters: Put story beginnings in a slice of bread at the bottom of the board. Build a sandwich using a variety of "ingredients"–pickle, tomato, lettuce, cheese and meat slices. Put story endings in another slice of bread and use to "top" each sandwich.

Tree Cluster

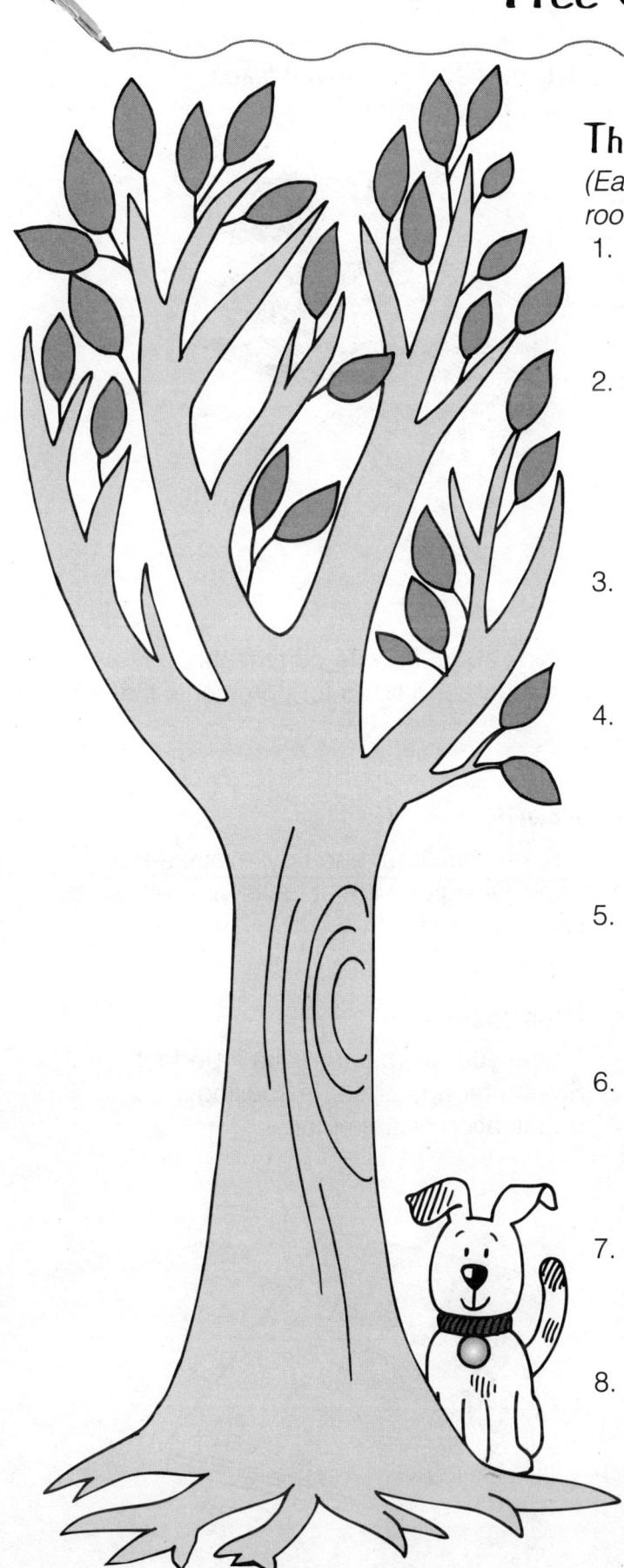

The Tree Trunk: My dog ran away.
(Each complete scenario below includes, in order, roots, trunk, branches, twigs and leaves.)

1. My dog got sprayed by a skunk; My dog ran away; We searched the woods near our house; We followed the smell of a skunk; We found my dog hiding in a bush.
2. My dog saw a cat and pulled his leash out of my hand; My dog ran away; I chased him and got lost; I found a Neighborhood Watch sign and knocked on the door; I called my mom from inside the house; My mom came and got me, and we found the dog on our way home.
3. There was a hole in our backyard fence; My dog ran away; We searched the neighborhood; We stayed out until 11:00 but could not find him; We went home, and he was waiting at our front door.
4. My dog was always barking at the new dog next door; My dog ran away; My neighbor's dog ran away; Another neighbor called to say the two dogs were hiding from the rain in his garage; My dog had puppies that looked like the dog next door.
5. My dog ate the garbage and got in trouble; My dog ran away; We put signs up around the neighborhood; We put an ad in the newspaper offering a reward; Someone called to say they had found my dog but didn't want the reward.
6. My dog got scared during a thunderstorm; My dog ran away; We called the dog pound; The people at the pound said they had a dog that looked like mine; We went to the pound and picked up my dog.
7. I dropped my dog; My dog ran away; I called and called, but he didn't come; I went to bed crying; I heard something else crying under my bed–it was my dog with a hurt paw.
8. We took my dog to the veterinarian; My dog ran away; He ran all around the vet's office; He scared all the other animals; A big dog started chasing him, and he ran into my arms.

The Writing Process

The writing process is a simple step-by-step formula that takes the mystery and confusion out of writing.

Pick and Plan
Pick your topic, collect information about your topic and then plan what you want your writing to tell about that topic.

Put It in Print
Write your first draft. Put all of your ideas on your paper. Don't worry about messiness, mistakes or mix-ups.

Revise
Now it's time to make your work better. Read it, think about it, write comments, reorganize, make changes, share the work with a friend and listen for comments that will improve your work.

Rewrite
Write a final, neat and tidy, mistake-free copy. Design so that it looks—as well as sounds—great.

Proofread
Refine your work and make it perfect. Search for any errors in spelling, punctuation or grammar.

Publish
Share your great work! Show it off to others by displaying it, passing it along or having it printed in a newsletter, newspaper or book.

Editing

Help students understand that it takes several drafts and many changes to reach the final stage of the writing process. Editing is an important part of the writing process.

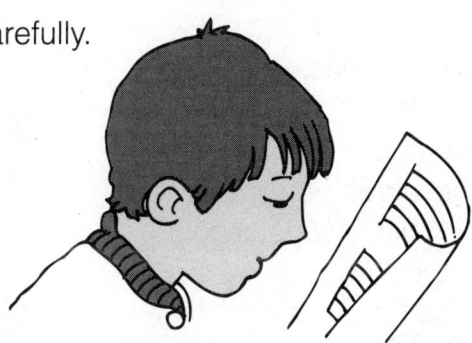

1. **Read** your work over very carefully.

2. **Think** about your work as you read it again. Draw a star beside the parts you like. Put a question mark beside parts that puzzle you or parts that may need some editing. Make some changes.

3. **Share** your work with a peer editor. Have your friend read it to you.

4. **Accept** helpful, constructive comments and criticism. Learn from the comments you receive.

5. **Make** changes.

6. **Reorganize** to make your work flow smoothly. Rearrange, change, substitute or add paragraphs and words. Add detail. Change endings. Make your beginning come alive.

7. **Rewrite** your work. Make changes according to the information you have gathered.

8. **Proofread.** Your work is now ready for proofreading.

Editing Center

Materials

- ✓ editing checklist
- ✓ punctuation and grammar guidebooks
- ✓ dictionary
- ✓ thesaurus
- ✓ pencils of various colors
- ✓ paper
- ✓ erasers
- ✓ sticky notes, paper clips
- ✓ pocket folders or writing folders

What to Do

1. Provide a space and materials that will promote the editing process.
2. Have children visit the center to revise and make use of resources.

"Check It Over" Checklist

- ✓ Read it over.
- ✓ Does it make sense.
- ✓ How does it look?
- ✓ Sound it out.
- ✓ Make it neat and tidy.

Editing Symbols

Circle spelling errors.
Box sections where punctuation is incorrect.
Underline sections that don't sound right.

The Goof-Proof Grammar Guide

Capitalize
- ✓ the first word in a sentence
- ✓ the first word of a direct quotation: The boy cried, "Wait for me!"
- ✓ special names of people, places and things: Illinois; Central Library
- ✓ proper nouns and adjectives: Abraham Lincoln; the English language
- ✓ words used as names: Mother; Granny
- ✓ people's titles with names: Queen Elizabeth; Dr. Johnson
- ✓ abbreviations or titles and groups: Mr.; NHL
- ✓ days, months and holidays: Tuesday, January, Christmas
- ✓ titles of books, movies, newspapers, poems and TV shows
- ✓ names of celestial bodies: the Milky Way
- ✓ names of geographic designations, streets and buildings: East 24th Street; Waverly House

Put a Period (.)
- ✓ at the end of a statement, a request, a command, a word that has been abbreviated–or when using decimals

Put a Question Mark (?)
- ✓ at the end of a question

Put an Exclamation Point (!)
- ✓ at the end of sentence that expresses strong emotion

Insert a Comma (,)
- ✓ in places where you want readers to pause
- ✓ to separate a series of three or more words
- ✓ in a letter after the greeting and the closing
- ✓ between a city and a state or province
- ✓ between the day, date and year
- ✓ to separate dialogue in a sentence
- ✓ after a word that you want to emphasize or an expression of emotion
- ✓ after the connecting words *or*, *and* and *but* in a compound sentence

Use an Apostrophe (')
- ✓ in contractions to take the place of missing letters (can't, I'm)
- ✓ to show ownership

    singular possessive*: the girl's book
    plural possessive**: the girls' books
    plural possessive: the children's books

    (*in proper nouns that end in *s*, the apostrophe comes after the *s* or before an added extra *s*: Jonas'; Jonas's)

    (**in nouns that do not end with *s*, an *s* must be added after the apostrophe: the children's books)

Place a Colon (:)
- ✓ between hours and minutes in written time (6:15)
- ✓ after the greeting in a business letter (Dear Mr. Read:)
- ✓ at the beginning of a list: My favorite stuffed toys are: Bunny, Bear, Giraffe and Horsey.

Put Quotation Marks (" ")
- ✓ around the words a person says or thinks
- ✓ on either side of a title or a slang word or phrase

Put a Hyphen (-)
- ✓ at the end of a syllable of a word when the word is continued on the next line: John ran right past the doc-tor. He didn't realize that
- ✓ between the numbers of written fractions: one-third

To Make a Singular Noun Plural
- ✓ add *s* to most words
- ✓ add *es* to words that end with *sh, ch, x, s* and *z*
- ✓ change *y* to *i* and add *es* to words that end in *y* and are preceded by a consonant
- ✓ change the spelling to create a new word for certain regular nouns: child . . . children

Abbreviations
- ✓ usually begin with a capital letter and end with a period: Mrs., Ave., St. There are exceptions, including: a.m., p.m.

Chapter 4

Write for a Reason

I Love Lists

Children use lists to organize their thoughts–and expand their vocabulary!

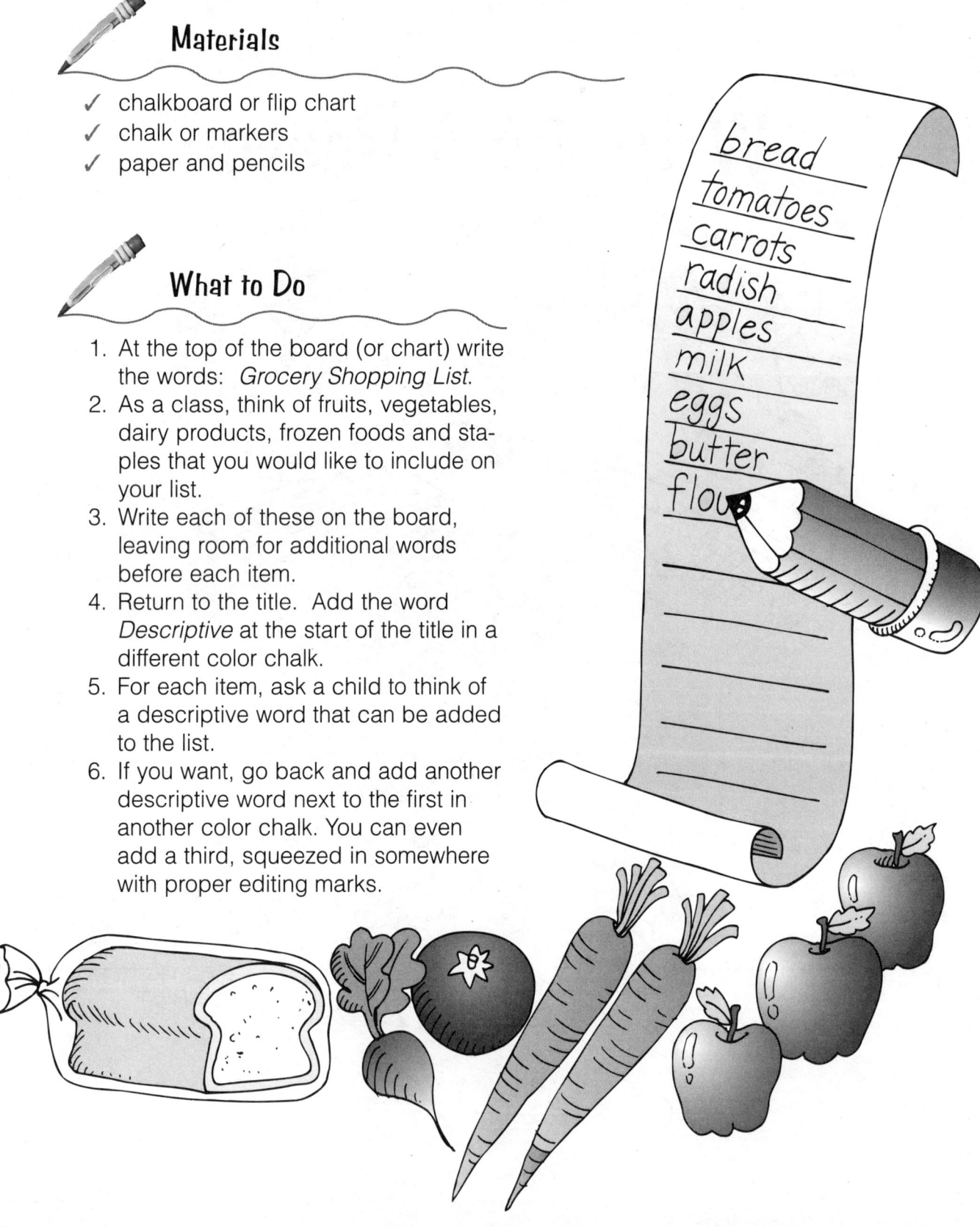

Materials

- ✓ chalkboard or flip chart
- ✓ chalk or markers
- ✓ paper and pencils

What to Do

1. At the top of the board (or chart) write the words: *Grocery Shopping List*.
2. As a class, think of fruits, vegetables, dairy products, frozen foods and staples that you would like to include on your list.
3. Write each of these on the board, leaving room for additional words before each item.
4. Return to the title. Add the word *Descriptive* at the start of the title in a different color chalk.
5. For each item, ask a child to think of a descriptive word that can be added to the list.
6. If you want, go back and add another descriptive word next to the first in another color chalk. You can even add a third, squeezed in somewhere with proper editing marks.

For example, where the order of addition is:
- ✓ **bold** (original word)
- ✓ <u>underline</u> (first addition)
- ✓ *italics* (second addition)
- ✓ [brackets] (third addition)

Tracey's [really cool] <u>DESCRIPTIVE</u> **GROCERY SHOPPING LIST**

<u>Ice</u> *cold* [refreshing] **milk**
fresh <u>white</u> [chicken's] **eggs**
thick <u>sliced</u> [brown] **bread**
old <u>cheddar</u> **cheese** [slices]
frozen [battered]) **fish** sticks
[juicy] <u>red</u> *Delicious* **apples**

Try This

- ✓ Make a descriptive Alliteration Alphabet Shopping List by organizing items in alphabetical order and using only descriptive words that start with the same letter as each item.
- ✓ Write a descriptive Christmas Wish List.
- ✓ Draft descriptive "To Do" Lists:
  - Get up (early); Brush (tangled) hair; Get dressed (quickly); Eat (hot) (oatmeal) breakfast; Catch (big) (yellow) (school) bus; etc.
  - Fix (clogged) drain; Wash (dirty) laundry; Clean (messy) room, etc.

How'd He Do That?

Developing step-by-step "how-to" instructions for the performance of simple, everyday tasks, children improve their analytical, organizational and descriptive skills.

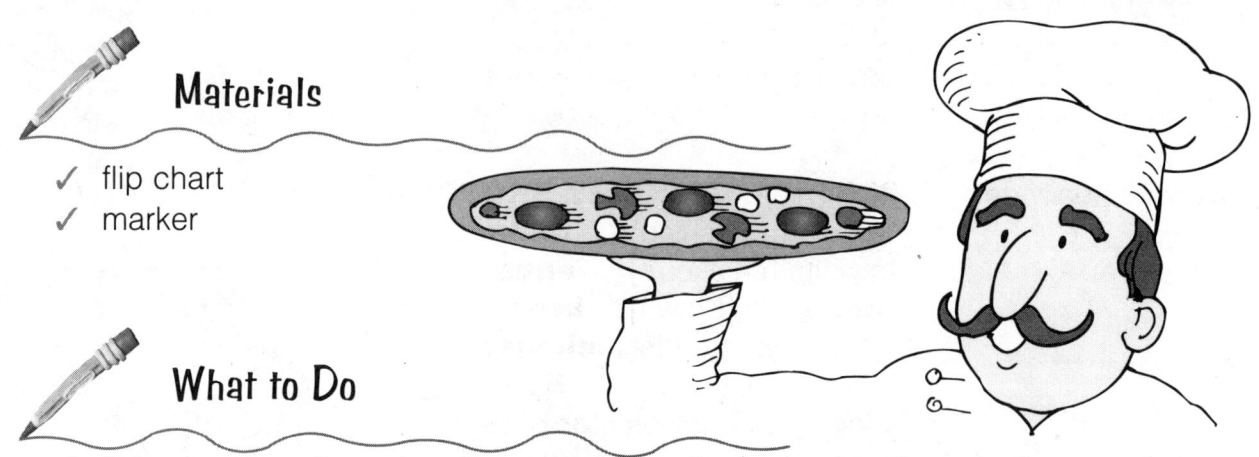

Materials

✓ flip chart
✓ marker

What to Do

1. Bring in a favorite recipe. Read the instructions aloud to illustrate the use of step-by-step directions in the "making" or "doing" of something. (Number the steps to show the correct order.)
2. As a class, choose a "simple" activity.
3. Have the children describe, in detail, the steps involved in completing the activity.
4. Write each "how-to" instruction on the flip chart.
5. Make sure that the instructions are detailed and accurate. The recipe was a simplified version of this how-to exercise. An alien visitor, with no knowledge of "Earth-type" things, should be able to follow your step-by-step directions and achieve the desired result. (See "Model Activity" on page 65.)
6. This is a lot more challenging than it sounds. The number of steps involved in carrying out even the simplest task–steps that we follow every day–is enormous. Have the children think carefully about each action and run through each step to make sure that their instructions are sufficient. Inevitably, a direction further down will point to a flaw in one above. Don't be afraid to make revisions and additions as you go along.
7. Trial the directions. Ask someone–either a student or an outside volunteer–to follow your instructions to the letter. Does she do what she is supposed to do, make what she is supposed to make or go where she is supposed to go? (If not, what steps should be clarified or added?)

Try This

✓ Have the students develop instruction lists for other activities–putting on a shirt, tying a shoelace, playing a sport or game, preparing a food.

How'd He Do That? Model Activity

Brushing Teeth

(assuming right-handedness and knowledge of bathroom, sink, tap, toothbrush, water, bristles . . . !)

1. Go to bathroom.
2. At sink, locate toothbrush and place, bristle side up, on counter.
3. Locate toothpaste.
4. Holding toothpaste tube in left hand, unscrew cap on toothpaste tube with right thumb and forefinger by twisting in a counterclockwise direction.
5. Place cap on counter.
6. Switch toothpaste tube to right hand.
7. Pick up toothbrush by placing left hand on brush handle.
8. Hold bristles adjacent to opening in toothpaste tube at 90°.
9. Place thumb on one side of toothpaste tube and other fingers on the other.
10. Squeeze toothpaste tube gently until ½" (1.25 cm) of paste is protruding from tube opening.
11. STOP SQUEEZING!
12. Transfer toothpaste from tube to brush by gently drawing toothbrush bristles across tube opening.
13. Carefully set toothbrush, bristle/paste side up, on counter.
14. Transferring tube to left hand, replace cap by grasping firmly between thumb and forefinger, pressing gently on tube neck and turning in clockwise direction until cap comes to rest.
15. Place tube on counter.
16. Grasp cold water tap (on right) with right hand and turn counterclockwise.
17. Grasp toothbrush handle in right hand and lift.
18. Place bristles beneath running tap water.
19. Wet thoroughly.
20. With left hand, turn tap clockwise to shut water off.
21. Raise toothbrush to mouth and pass bristles in front of and behind upper and lower teeth with short, up-and-down strokes.
22. Pass bristles over upper and lower back teeth (on cheek and tongue side) with an up-and-down and sawing (or back-and-forth) motion.
23. DO NOT SWALLOW TOOTHPASTE LATHER.
24. Continue these motions for two minutes.
25. With left hand, turn tap counterclockwise to start water flow.
26. Remove toothbrush from mouth and hold beneath running tap water to rinse.
27. Return toothbrush to original position.
28. Lean head over sink and spit toothpaste lather into drain.
29. Place lips beneath nozzle and allow water to flow into mouth.
30. DO NOT SWALLOW.
31. Use cheek muscles to move water around inside mouth to rinse.
32. Spit rinse water into sink.
33. If desired, place lips to water and fill mouth again.
34. Close lips.
35. Raise head.
36. Swallow.

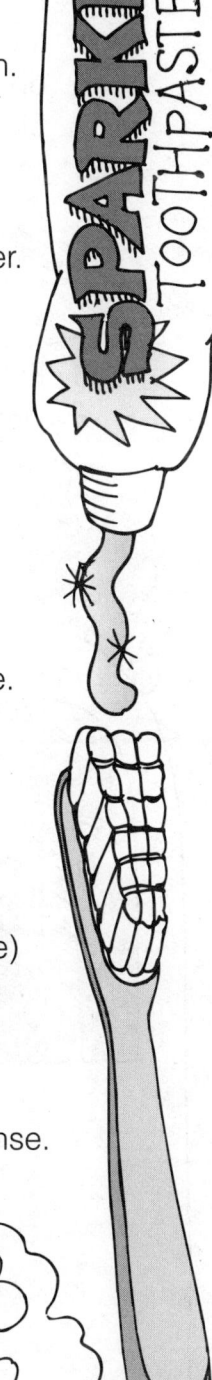

Write a Letter

Children use their writing skills to communicate a formal message.

Materials

✓ model format letters
✓ letter writing paper, envelopes and writing tools
✓ optional copy of *Free Stuff for Kids*, Editor Judi Peers, Stoddart Publishing Co. Limited, current edition

What to Do

1. Provide students with model letters. Talk about the format of these samples.
2. Have students write their own letters.

Informal Sample Letter

23 Burns Street
Mapleton, ON K0A 1G0
January 1, 2000

Dear Emma,

    I was so happy to hear that you will be coming for a visit. I don't know if I can wait until March! I hope that you can bring your puppy with you. I would love to see her too.

    I will have the ponies waiting in the barn when you arrive. We can take the old wagon road out to the meadow. Maybe we will see Smokey on the way.

    Have a safe trip.

    Your friend,

    Jenni

P.S. Don't forget your riding helmet!

Formal Sample Letter

Stephanie Matson
44 Everett St.
Pleasanton, CA 94551
May 30, 1999

Mr. P. Jones
Hands for Seniors Organization
321 Roebuck Dr.
San Jose, CA 94451

Dear Mr. Jones:

I read in the newspaper that you were looking for some children to help take care of gardens for seniors this summer. I am interested in helping with this project.

I am 15 years old and have worked in my family's gardens for many years. I have helped some of my neighbors and my grandparents with their gardens, too. I have a lot of books on the subject and think that I could do a good job.

My mother and father are willing to drive me to the gardens and have offered to supervise once a week.

I hope to hear from you soon.

Sincerely,

Stephanie Matson

Research and Report

Do you have questions about the world?
Do you want to know more about something that interests you?
Put your reading and writing skills to good use, and find out something you always wanted to know!

Materials

- ✓ index cards (10 for each student)
- ✓ research materials: books, newspapers, computer resources, library
- ✓ writing tools (paper and pencil, computer and printer)

Writing a Report

Lead students through the report-writing process.

What to Do

1. Have students choose a topic of interest.
2. What do they want to know about the subject? Have students make a list of three to five questions.
3. There is lots of information out there! Start your search!
4. Help students to:
   - ✓ search through library books, encyclopedias and magazines
   - ✓ take notes from a movie or filmstrip
   - ✓ log on to a computer to check out an informative CD-ROM or the internet
   - ✓ ask teachers, friends, family or specialists in the community
5. Help students record one piece of information on each index card. Students can record in point form.
6. Help students organize their information.
7. Lay the index cards out on a table.
8. Group cards together that they answer the same question.
9. Organize information so there is a beginning, middle and end.*
10. Prepare the rough draft.

Check It Over

Read the report out loud.
Is it organized?
Does it have a beginning, middle and end?*
Does it make sense?
A teacher or parent should proofread for spelling and punctuation.

Add the Finishing Touches

Are you going to add illustrations, diagrams or pictures from a magazine or computer program?
If so, plan where these materials will fit into your report.

Write the Final Copy

Rewrite your report in your best handwriting or type it on your computer and print it out. Add diagrams and pictures.
Add a title page and a cover if you wish.

*Beginning, Middle and End

The Beginning

A beginning or opening paragraph should tell readers what your report is about and capture readers' interest so they want to read on. Writers can ask a question or tell an interesting detail.

The Middle

This part of your report will tell readers most of the information you have discovered.

The End

The final paragraph should wrap up the report in an interesting way. Finish with a question, a personal comment or a final interesting detail that was saved for the end.

Research and Report Checklist

- ❏ Pick a subject.

- ❏ Write some questions.

- ❏ Find some answers.

- ❏ Record your answers.

- ❏ Write a rough draft
  (make sure to include a beginning, middle and end).

- ❏ Edit your rough copy.

- ❏ Ask someone to check it over.

- ❏ Reedit.

- ❏ Proofread for errors.

- ❏ Plan your final copy.

- ❏ Write your final copy.

Whether you write fiction or nonfiction, the more research you do–the better your story will be. Details will be more exciting, settings will be more realistic, characters and plots will be more believable. You can find interesting facts in history books, travel guides, atlases and maps, newspapers and magazines, letters, journals, diaries, photo albums–even dictionaries!

Genres

Expose children to different genres of writing.

Different styles or kinds of writing are called writing "genres." There are two main genres: fiction and nonfiction. Within these two, there are many other genres, including: short stories, myths, legends, fairy tales, narratives, biographies, essays, fantasy, science and historical fiction. Children in grades 4-6 can discern the subtleties that separate one form of writing from another. Recognizing the patterns and rules that define a particular genre will provide young writers with a framework for their own writing.

Fiction Genres

Fiction is the name given to works about imagined happenings; things that are not true. These stories may contain elements of truth but are basically invented by the writer. This grouping of works contains short stories, adventure, romance and fantasy novels, picture books, mystery stories, poetry and plays.

Nonfiction Genres

The nonfiction genre includes forms of writing that deal with real-life facts and true happenings. Nonfiction works include magazine and newspaper articles, how-to books, textbooks, biographies, cookbooks, children's information books and more.

Explore Genres

Share several books of the same genre, maybe adventure or mystery novels. Read some of the best available materials in that particular genre. Check award lists and the classics for the top picks. Search for patterns and unifying elements in these books. Chart the commonalties between these works. Have students try their hand at writing in this framework.

Write a Children's Book

1. Choose an age and make some notes about that age group.
2. Choose fiction or nonfiction.
3. Decide upon the subject of interest. Look at your subject from the eyes of your target reader. (Remember, children generally like to read books about kids who are a few years older than they are.)
4. What writing style will make the topic interesting?
5. Consider using a light, funny tone or a cast of intriguing characters.
6. Make use of neat sidebars and illustrations in nonfiction works. Whatever you choose to do, make it interesting!
7. Choose a length for your work.
8. Find samples of similar works. Compare these books; make notes.
9. Notice the format, the layout, the size and length, the use of illustration and vocabulary and the tone.
10. Collect information on your subject.
11. Decide how you want to present this information. Make a storyboard and plan your format. Only the title of the chapters or a simple key word phrase needs to be placed on the pages of the "board." Use thumbnail sketches or brief descriptions in place of illustrations.
12. Write a rough draft. Number your written pages to correspond to your storyboard layout.
13. Edit and rewrite.
14. Add the finishing touches and write your final copy.
15. Add your illustrations, and then put your book together in book form.
16. Add a title page and a proper cover. Presto! You have made a children's picture book!

Get to Know a Writer

You don't have to meet an author to get to know one. Focus on a particular author's works and find out what you can about that author. You can usually obtain information about popular authors from libraries, bookstores, the publishers and writers' organizations. Provide your students with newspaper and magazine articles, biographical sketches found in books or offered by publishers and information presented on the internet. (If possible, book the author to visit, write to the author or make contact via e-mail or an on-line chat room.)

Getting "to know" an author will help students understand what it takes to be a good writer and how to recognize elements of a book that are unique to particular authors and genres. Recognizing the subtleties of written work will help students improve their own pieces.

Writers write about specific subjects, for specific audiences and for specific purposes. Each has a unique way of saying things, a distinctive vocabulary or a favorite plot. When students become familiar with an author's works, they develop an understanding of what to expect when they "go back for more." Eventually, they will be able to identify favorite authors just by listening to a few passages of a new book.

Activity

- ✓ Share two or more books by a popular author.
- ✓ Record students' comments about the works.
- ✓ What makes this writer's work unique?
- ✓ Read passages from books by various familiar authors. Do not disclose the author's identity. Can students recognize the writers by their styles?

Chapter 5

Story Makers

Say It Your Own Way

Just as each person has his own way of saying things, so too, does he have his own way of expressing himself in writing. Every writer is empowered with a uniqueness that allows her to choose words and weave them in her own distinctive way according to her imagination and experiences. By grade 4, students might be starting to recognize their own unique style of writing, their favorite genre, their own language and their own writer's voice.

With experience, writers will develop their own unique voice. This will show itself in the form of vocabulary, sense of humor, characterization, dialogue, subject, setting, narrative structure and plot.

Materials

- ✓ paragraph from a novel your class is sharing
- ✓ news item from the local newspaper
- ✓ event that happened in your classroom

What to Do

1. Provide students with a piece of writing, or describe an event.
2. Have each student write her own version of the material. Encourage students to "say it their way."
3. Have students share their interpretations. Discuss style differences, and distinctions in the methods used to communicate events, feelings and ideas.

Story Builders

*In this cooperative activity children build a story together
using the thoughts of their classmates as inspiration for their own.*

Materials

- ✓ chalkboard or flip chart
- ✓ chalk or markers
- ✓ paper and pencils

What to Do

1. To build a story as a group, write an opening sentence on the board or chart. This might be: "Once upon a time there was a little fairy dog named Sissy." or "One day a grand piano fell out of a second story window and crushed Mr. McQuerter's brand-new red Cadillac Seville," or "Karen was in big trouble." (Try to make it interesting–even unusual –but not necessarily silly. The best stories are the ones that make sense.)
2. Go around the classroom asking each child in turn to add a complete sentence to the story.
3. Bring the story to a natural conclusion, either with a child's sentence or one of your own, after everyone has had a turn.
4. Read the story back.
5. Break into small groups of two or three and build new stories on paper.
6. Have the groups read their stories out loud. (The groups can choose a reader, or each member can read her own sentences.)

Try This

- ✓ Here is a silly way to build a story. It won't produce Pulitzer Prize-winning material, but it does get kids laughing and writing. In small groups, have one person write a story starter at the top of a blank piece of paper. This time, the sentence should be left incomplete. "Once upon a time there was a . . ." or "One day a grand piano . . ." Fold the top of the paper down so it covers and hides the sentence. The story starter must then write the next word of the sentence on a new line: *fairy* in the first case and *fell* in the second. The next person must pick up at this point and continue the story, ending his turn in the same way as the story starter. (There will have to be the occasional period, so ask the children to finish a sentence and start a new one every now and then.) Continue writing until the story wraps itself up.

Story Starters

Children learn how to develop a story around the key elements of setting, character and plot.

Materials

- ✓ "Story Starters List" (page 79)
- ✓ flip chart and marker
- ✓ paper
- ✓ pencils

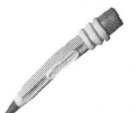

What to Do

1. As a group, choose one item from each of the three categories in the Story Starters List: Setting, Character and Plot.
2. Together, create a short story based on the three story elements.
3. After the group demonstration, have the children choose three different items from the list and create a short story of their own. (Encourage use of the Clustering techniques on page 54 to flesh out story outlines.)
4. Read the stories aloud.

Try This

- ✓ Have the children use the same three story starter elements. When the stories are completed, read and compare.
- ✓ Encourage the children to choose three items not on the list.
- ✓ Use the story starters as a timed writing exercise (description on page 43). There are several ways to do this:
    - Have the children write a complete short story.
    - Have the children write the first paragraph of a longer, more detailed piece of writing. (All items must be included in this story starter.)
    - Choose three items "blindfolded" and have the children write about the same thing (either complete stories or first paragraphs). Read and compare as above.

Story Starters List

Setting

- ✓ pirate ship
- ✓ gangster hideout
- ✓ school
- ✓ witch's lair
- ✓ playground
- ✓ toy store
- ✓ amusement park
- ✓ beach
- ✓ submarine
- ✓ factory

Character

- ✓ girl/boy
- ✓ giant
- ✓ witch
- ✓ baseball player
- ✓ animal
- ✓ TV or movie star
- ✓ bank robber
- ✓ inventor
- ✓ spy/detective
- ✓ magician

Plot

- ✓ explosion
- ✓ magic spell
- ✓ lost in the woods
- ✓ caught in a hurricane
- ✓ fight with a bully
- ✓ hunt for lost treasure
- ✓ escape from a villain
- ✓ battle with aliens
- ✓ find a stray animal
- ✓ lose a favorite possession

What a Character!

In these "character building" exercises, children learn to create life on paper and to give their stories a main character they will never forget.

Materials

- ✓ characterization exercises
- ✓ pencils and paper
- ✓ newspaper obituary

Get Ready

1. Discuss characterization with the students.
   (*Central to every good story is a good main character. The writer must know this character intimately and understand him completely: how he looks, acts and feels; what he thinks, eats, wears; who he loves, likes, hates. To the writer, this character is a close friend, so close that she knows him as well as she knows herself. A character is not convincing unless the author can get inside his head and take the reader with him. Developing a character sketch is a good way for a writer to get to know his character.*)
2. Write the character prompts in Frankenstein's Monster on the board.
3. Explain that when devising a character sketch, writers are like Dr. Frankenstein: they have the ability to create life–on paper anyway!
4. To create their own monsters, have the students complete the Frankenstein's Monster character sketch, adding any additional information that comes to mind.

Frankenstein

big	scary	gigantic
cu...	gentle	ugly
	tall	curious
	sensitive	clumsy

Frankenstein's Monster Character Sketch

- ✓ name
- ✓ physical/description
- ✓ strengths/weaknesses
- ✓ family members/pets/best friend/worst enemy and relationships with each
- ✓ interests/hobbies/favorite sports/pastimes
- ✓ things that make the character happy, sad, angry, frightened, annoyed, etc.
- ✓ things the character loves/hates the most
- ✓ emotional characteristics (shy, aggressive, self-confident, bullying, etc.)
- ✓ attitude toward school/homework/life in general
- ✓ exclusive favorite expression ("As if!" "Whatever!" "Yahooee!" "I don't think so.")
- ✓ exclusive annoying habit (hair twirling, knee bouncing, nail biting, eye rolling?)

Easy Epithets

What to Do

1. Have the children write an epithet to describe their character. (An epithet is a term, word or phrase used to characterize a person or a thing.)
   Gary, for example, could be "One heck of a guy!"
   Tracey (see below), simply, "Loner."
2. Have the children write epithets for one another. (These must be positive characterizations!)

Knock Knock. Who's There?

In this guessing game, children give and receive descriptive character clues to uncover the identity of a mystery guest.

What to Do

1. Have one child go into the hall.
2. Give this child a "secret identity" (doctor, teacher, amusement park operator, hotel guest, King Kong, Queen of England . . .)
3. Tell the student to think about his character and knock on the door when ready.
4. Once invited into the classroom, he begins answering questions posed by the other students and designed to discover his identity.
5. The "mystery" student can answer questions with only: "yes," "no" or "maybe."
6. Impose a time or question limit.
7. When the limit is reached, the mystery guest then offers clues to his classmates regarding his identity until someone guesses correctly.

Try This

✓ Play the game in reverse. When the student is in the hall, tell the class her mystery identity. She must then enter the class and try to discover her own identity by asking questions of the other students. The same rules apply as above.

From the Outside In

What to Do

1. Have the children write a description that examines a character from the inside out (or the outside in!). For the outer perspective, describe physical characteristics: what the character is and does. For the inner perspective, describe emotional characteristics: who the character is and how she feels. (These descriptions should be written in paragraph form and should flow together naturally.)
2. Have the children read their favorite descriptions out loud.

Outside–What she is:
Tracey is a tall girl for her age, willowy and awkward. She has a strange, limping way of walking. She is neither ugly, nor pretty, but oddly nondescript. With her untamed, long brown hair and her eyes like dark chocolate peering out from behind thick, gold rimmed glasses, she looks like an old soul in a young girl's body.

Outside–What she does:
At recess, Tracey sits on the front steps of the school, her nose in a book and her knee bouncing rapidly up and down. She always has her homework done and she is the favorite of all her teachers. She is a member of the library club, the computer club, the chess club, the camera club and the yearbook committee, but she has never made the cut for a single school team.

Inside–Who she is:
She is one of those smart kids that average kids call "keener" and below average kids call "brainer." She is a loner, not because she chooses to be one, but because she is destined to be one. She eats alone, she reads alone and she walks alone and yet, she is not alone. She keeps company with some of the most adventurous children of all time: children like Tom Sawyer and Huck Finn; Mowgli the Man Cub; Nancy Drew and the Hardy boys.

Inside–How she feels:
From time to time, Tracey experiences a penetrating loneliness. When this happens, she feels cut off from everything that lives and breathes. Her own breathing becomes shallow; her heart is too heavy with sorrow to bother oxygenating. She feels light-headed. At these times, she cannot go to school. She feels a momentary brightening when someone arrives with the work her teachers have sent home. She never answers the door.

Dr. Jeckle and Mr. Hyde: An Alter Ego Exercise

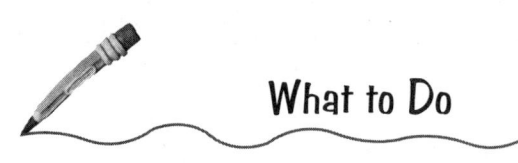

What to Do

1. Write the following paragraph on the board:
    Gary was a super person. Everybody loved him and he loved everybody. He was friendly and generous to everyone he met and kind to animals. He was a perfect gentleman and an incredible human being. He had a way of bringing out the best in people.
2. As a group, create Gary's alter ego–the person who is Gary's complete opposite; good Dr. Jeckle's evil Mr. Hyde–by changing each sentence from positive to negative. Write these sentences on the board. When you are finished, it might look something like this:
    Yrag* was a horrible person. Everybody hated him and he hated everybody. He was mean and miserly with everyone he met and cruel to animals. He was an absolute villain and a repulsive human being. He had a way of bringing out the worst in people.
    * "Yrag" is "Gary" backwards.
3. Have the children write a few descriptive lines about a nice person. Then ask them to create their good character's alter ego.
4. Reverse the exercise. Go from Mr. Hyde to Dr. Jeckle.

Descriptive Obits

What to Do

1. Cut out an obituary from the newspaper. (Obituaries are excellent mini character sketches and a great source for character inspiration.)
2. Photocopy the obituary and give one copy to each child.
3. Have students read the obituary to themselves and then create another paragraph that further describes the individual being remembered. Give lots of detail.
4. Write a paragraph that shows the darker side of the person–stuff that wouldn't be found in an obituary. No human being is all saint or all sinner.
5. Ask the children to read their additions aloud.
6. Have the children create their own obituaries, perhaps about a relative or friend who has passed away.

Try This

✓ Create the alter ego of the person described in the obituary. (See Dr. Jeckle and Mr. Hyde on page 84.)
✓ Write an epitaph–the inscription on a tombstone–for one of your characters.
   "Cary Granite: Pillar of the community; Rock of Gibraltar."
   "Erin Areways, beloved husband of Judy: Here lies Erin, brokenhearted.
       Sickly since the day she parted."

Point of View: Who's Story Is This?

Children learn the difficult concept of "point of view" by completing an exercise that compares the first, second, third and fourth person.

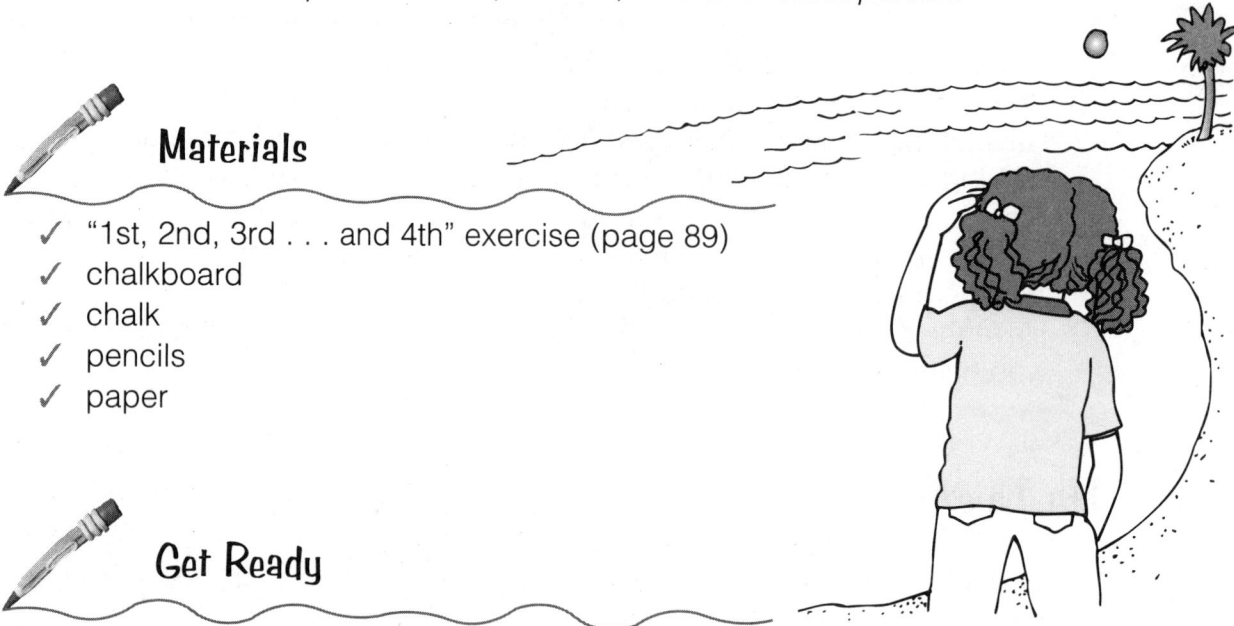

Materials

- ✓ "1st, 2nd, 3rd . . . and 4th" exercise (page 89)
- ✓ chalkboard
- ✓ chalk
- ✓ pencils
- ✓ paper

Get Ready

Talk to the children about first, second and third person and the ways in which "point of view" shapes a story.

Every story has to have someone to tell it. In some cases, it is the author. When the author tells us someone else's story, we say he is writing in the "third person." In some cases, the author lets the main character tell the story. When the character is allowed to speak for herself, the author is writing in the "first person." Very occasionally, an author will write in the "second person" and tell the reader's own story.

*(There is a little used "fourth person." In this kind of story, the author uses an all-knowing, all-seeing or "omniscient" narrator to talk to the reader. This narrator knows everything that has, does and will happen to all of the characters and talks freely to the reader about all of them, using "transporting" words such as **meanwhile** to flit between characters. A story written in the fourth person has a magical, fairy tale or surreal feel to it. Not surprisingly, it is an omniscient narrator that tells the "once upon a time" stories.)*

Before you can write a story, you have to decide who is going to tell it and who it is going to be about. Will you tell your main character's story? Will you let your main character tell her own story? Will you tell your reader a story about himself? Or, will you let someone else talk directly to your reader and tell the story of a group of people? In other words, before you can write a story, you have to decide from whose point of view the story will be told.

You can choose to tell your story from whatever point of view you want, just make sure that the voice you use comes naturally and suits your story. Once you have chosen a voice, you MUST stick with it. With the exception of a story written in the fourth person, you cannot jump around from one point of view to another. You must stay inside your character's head at all times. You can only hear what your character hears, see what your character sees and think what your character thinks. Your character cannot know what other people are thinking, doing or experiencing; she can only imagine it or hear about it in conversation.

(The only exception to this rule is if you write a story that features different characters in different chapters. This is like telling two or more stories in the same book. Each chapter must be clearly labeled with the character's name, so we know who "owns" the chapter and from whose point of view the story will be told. With this technique, different characters can tell the same story from different perspectives, or pick up the narrative thread of a single story, adding on to the tale where the previous character left off. This technique should be used only if it is absolutely necessary for the reader to know what is going on in the heads of a number of different people.)

Write these examples on the board and discuss the use of first, second and third person and the different points of view.
1. I like animals. My family has a dog. Our dog's name is Brandy. Brandy is mine and she loves me.
2. You like animals. Your family has a dog. Your dog's name is Brandy. Brandy is yours and she loves you.
3. Julia likes animals. Her family has a dog. Their dog's name is Brandy. Brandy is hers and she loves her.

In the first example, the author is letting the main character tell her story. Use of the words *I, my, our, me* and *mine* tells us that this story is written in the first person.

In the second example, the author is speaking directly to the reader. By using the words *you* and *your*, she shows us that she is writing in the second tense.

In the third example, the author is talking about Tracey. Her use of Tracey's name and the words *her, hers* and *their* tells us that the story is written in the third person. Most writers use the third person to tell their stories.

TLC10203 Copyright © Teaching & Learning Company, Carthage, IL 62321-0010

1st, 2nd, 3rd . . . and 4th

What to Do

1. Write the following paragraph on the board:

   His name is Charles Darwin.

   His name is Charles Darwin–his parents named him after "that famous natural selection guy"–but most people call him "derWinner." He doesn't mind. He knows it's a German joke and thinks it kind of suits him. Charles' teachers call him the "class clown" and give him really bad marks on his report card under the "attitude" section, but the kids think he's funny and he thinks that's cool. He really likes to make people laugh. It makes him feel good about himself. He's already worked up about a hundred stand-up comedy routines, and someday Charles is going to be a professional comedian and put all that "bad attitude" to good use. Right now, he's just practicing.

2. Taking turns, have the children change the paragraph from the third person into the first person. Read out each sentence (or sentence fragment) before the child attempts to change it.
3. Write each new sentence on the board.
4. When the paragraph is complete, read it aloud. It will look something like this:

   My name is Charles Darwin–my parents named me after that famous "natural selection" guy–but most people call me "derWinner." I don't mind. It's kind of a German joke, and I think it kind of suits me. My teachers call me the "class clown" and give me really bad marks on my report card under the "attitude" section, but the kids think I'm funny and I think that's cool. I really like to make people laugh. It makes me feel good about myself. I've already worked up about a hundred stand-up comedy routines, and someday I'm going to be a professional comedian and put all that "bad attitude" to good use. Right now, I'm just practicing.

   My name is Charles Darwin.

5. Following the same pattern as above, change the paragraph to the second person. It will look like this:

Your real name is Charles Darwin–your parents named you after that famous "natural selection guy"–but most people call you "derWinner." You don't mind. You know it's a German joke, and you think it kind of suits you. Your teachers call you the "class clown" and give you really bad marks on your report card under the "attitude" section, but the kids think you're funny and you think that's cool. You really like to make people laugh. It makes you feel good about yourself. You have already worked up about a hundred stand-up comedy routines, and someday you are going to be a professional comedian and put all that "bad attitude" to good use. Right now, you're just practicing.

6. Finally, change the paragraph to the fourth person. This is not a simple pronoun substitution exercise. It will have to be substantially rewritten. Use this as an example or by way of comparison to illustrate how subjective this particular conversion is:

Once upon a time, there was a young boy named Charles Darwin. His parents, who were both fanatical natural historians, named him after their hero: the famous scientist, Charles Darwin, who developed the theory of natural selection. Charles was a prankster and very poor at language arts, and most of his friends called him "derWinner" by way of a friendly joke. Charles loved to make people laugh, and while all the children delighted in his keen sense of humor, his teachers (who were secretly jealous of Charles' wild popularity) deemed it distracting and unacceptable. They punished Charles by him making him wear a dunce hat labelled, **Class Clown***, at recess time and giving him undeservedly poor marks on his report cards. But Charles would not be put off. He dreamed of becoming a stand-up comedian, and he practiced his outrageous slapstick routines every night before a mirror in the sanctuary of his bedroom.*

7. Have the children develop their own paragraphs using one of the four points of view.
8. Then ask them to trade paragraphs and change the point of view.
9. Which "person" do the children feel most comfortable using in their stories? Which do they think works the best for the "derWinner" story? Discuss how point of view changes the feel of a story like "derWinner."

Choosing a Setting

In this descriptive exercise, children re-create their own surroundings or invent a setting that might serve as the backdrop for a story.

Materials

✓ pencils and paper

Get Ready

Discuss setting with the children.
(Although they are well disguised, the five Ws are the building blocks of all stories. The "Whos" are the characters; the "Whats" are their problems. But what about the "Whens" and "Wheres"? Every story–fact, fiction or fantasy– has to be situated somewhere. Stories can take place in the past, present or future (yesterday, today or tomorrow), and they can be situated in real or imaginary places. Where will your story take place? In your neighborhood or school? In the darkest jungles of Africa or the frigid far north? On an airplane or a planet millions of light years from Earth?)

What to Do

1. To help them to more fully understand their own setting, have the children write about everything they heard, saw, tasted, smelled, touched and otherwise experienced on their way to the classroom. (Because we know it the best, our own setting is often the easiest one to use in a story.)
2. Then choose a different setting. Describe the physical characteristics of the place and its social environment. My setting is a warehouse:

It was dark and cold and misty, and the air settled around my shoulders like a wet towel. The warehouse was close to the ocean–in the water district–and there was a pervasive smell of fish and garbage and homelessness. A filthy blanket and an empty pack of cigarettes kept each other company in a dank corner. Gasoline lay in rainbow puddles on the concrete floor, and my footsteps echoed up into the rafters like the hollow voices of lost souls. Wooden crates were piled from floor to ceiling on either side of a narrow aisle. Faded letters decorated their sides, hinting at ancient voyages: Hong Kong, China; Sau Paulo, Brazil. A forklift jammed the aisle, its metal teeth piercing a particularly weathered crate.

Repetition

Children use a repeated word to establish setting.

A setting also has a particular feel to it. One way to create a feeling or mood is to use a trick called "repetition." To do this, writers focus on a single word and use it repeatedly in a single paragraph. Linked to other thoughts and images, the repetition never becomes boring to the reader, but rather enhances his concept of time and place.

Snow everywhere. Snow lying on the ground like a thick woolen blanket. Snow on the eves: white hats on furrowed black brows. Treacherous snow creeping stealthily onto slippery painted wooden porches. Snow on the railings and window ledges. Snow on the pathway where early morning footprints are like an angel's wings in powder clouds. Snow on my shovel, blowing back into my face on a sudden updraft like ashes from a wintry grate. Snow in the street muffling the sound of cars as they explore the old road for the first time, navigating slowly, cautiously, through a foreign and dangerous country. Snow on my mittens, crusty from sweat. Snow on the dog's nose rooting along the curb for a familiar, anchoring scent in an unfamiliar landscape.

What to Do

1. Choose an image: a feeling, a person, place or thing, a season.
2. Have the children use the word as many times and in as many ways as they can in the course of one or two paragraphs.
3. Share the paragraphs out loud. (One hundred people could write about the same thing and yet, because they each have their own unique experiences and particular point of view to bring to the story, every piece of writing would be different.)

Stacking

Children pile up images to describe a favorite or familiar place.

Another way to create a setting is to stack different images on top of one another in the description of a single place.

The junkyard is full of discarded history, worldly possessions shrugged off by the dead or the embarrassed. An old toaster, the cable frayed and singed. A doll without a head. Moldy books with rotten pages. Cracked buckets, broken shovels, legless chairs and tarnished cutlery. A highchair without a tray. Bicycle wheels, missing spokes, bald without tires. A ladder leans against the edge of the eclectic pit, promising access to collectors and curious. A ripped mattress, stained yellow in the middle, is home to a family of squirrels. Old fridges, old stoves and old freezers yawn open, their doors hanging from decrepit hinges. Here and there a salvageable treasure: a tin cup without a handle a carriage without a bonnet.

What to Do

1. As a group, brainstorm a list of items that could be found in a particular place.
2. Have each student add a sentence using one or more of the objects and images on the list. (Encourage "poetic" turns of phrase.)
3. Write down each sentence.
4. When the paragraph is complete, read it aloud.

Try This

✓ Have the children work individually with the brainstorming list, incorporating as many of the images as possible in their own paragraphs.
✓ Provide a new setting or ask the children to think of a place they would like to explore in an image-filled paragraph.

Getting Tense

In this exercise, children develop a sense of time–past, present and future–as well as an understanding of verb tenses and the way these alter both our writing and our thinking.

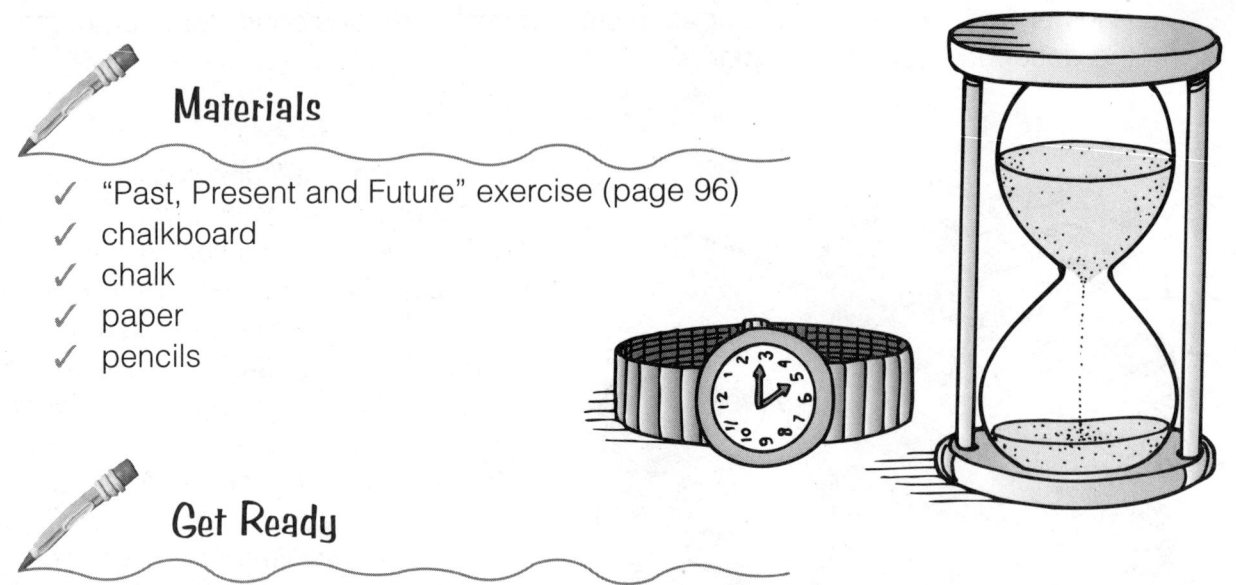

Materials

- ✓ "Past, Present and Future" exercise (page 96)
- ✓ chalkboard
- ✓ chalk
- ✓ paper
- ✓ pencils

Get Ready

Talk to the children about our sense of "time"–past, present and future–as a point of reference in our writing, in our speech and in our lives.

As long as we are alive, every human being has a past, a present and a future. Things happened to us in the past, they will happen to us in the future and at present, they are happening to us right now. Write these three sentences on the board and consider:

Jonathan went to the beach.
Jonathan is at the beach.
Jonathan is going to the beach.

In the first sentence, Jonathan has already been to the beach. This action happened sometime in the past. In the second sentence, Jonathan is at the beach right now, even as we are reading about him. In the third sentence, Jonathan–at some time in the future–will go to the beach. It is the verb in each sentence–the action word–that is altered: *went* in the past changes to *is at* in the present and then to *is going* in the future. If, in another sentence, "Joanna looks at Sally" in the present tense; then you can be sure that she "looked at Sally" in the past, and she "will look at Sally" in the future. A verb always changes with time.

Most stories are written in what we call the "past tense." They happened sometime in the past. In a way, we are "old news"–which is fine because it's old news that we haven't heard yet, and so it is still interesting. Even stories that start out in the "present tense," or the "here and now," often revert quickly to past tense. It is easier for most people to write about how something happened rather than how it is happening. For example, lots of stories start out like this:

> *I am kind of a teacher's pet, and I don't usually get into trouble, but last week I did something that got me grounded for the whole summer. It all started one rainy Saturday afternoon. I was . . ."*

See? I went from present tense–I am–to past tense–I was.

You can write in the present tense all the way through a story, but it is hard to sustain. If you did, it might sound something like this:

> *Stephanie is lying again. And like usual, she is trying to postpone the inevitable: the moment when her mother will discover the truth.*
>
> *"Mom?" she says in her most innocently startled voice. "I just remembered I have to call Katy about our French project. Can we talk about this missing test thing at dinnertime?"*
>
> *"Sure," says her mom, all sweetness and sympathy. "It's dinnertime."*

The future is definitely too hard to sustain:

> *"What will I do? I know I can trust Jennifer's mom, but what about her dad? If he finds out the truth, I'm sunk."*

It's not bad for one paragraph–when a character is projecting from her present state into the future, for example–but for a whole story?

Past, Present and Future

What to Do

1. Write the following paragraph on the board:
   Tom was mortified. He felt the hot, red fever of humiliation as it rushed up his neck and flooded into his face. The room began to spin. He sensed, rather than saw, Stacie's eyes on his back. They were boring a hole through his shirt and straight into his soul. He felt like crawling into a little hole. He felt like jumping off a cliff. He felt like throwing up.
2. Taking turns, have the children change the paragraph into the present tense. Read aloud each sentence (or sentence fragment) before the child attempts to change it.
3. Write each new sentence on the board.
4. When the paragraph is complete, read it aloud. It will look something like this:
   Tom is mortified. He feels the hot, red fever of humiliation as it rushes up his neck and floods into his face. The room begins to spin. He senses, rather than sees, Stacie's eyes on his back. They are boring a hole through his shirt and straight into his soul. He feels like crawling into a little hole. He feels like jumping off a cliff. He feels like throwing up.
5. Just for fun–and to illustrate a point–change the paragraph into the future tense.
   Tom will be mortified. He will feel the hot, red fever of humiliation as it rushes up his neck and floods into his face. The room will begin to spin. He will sense, rather than see, Stacie's eyes on his back. They will be boring a hole through his shirt and straight into his soul. He will feel like crawling into a little hole. He will feel like jumping off a cliff. He will feel like throwing up.
6. Circle the verbs in each paragraph. Talk about the way they are transformed as you switch from one tense to another.
7. Have the children develop their own paragraphs in one of the three tenses. Trade paragraphs and transform.

Look Who's Talking

The next few exercises are designed to familiarize kids with dialogue: how it is used and when it is used.

Materials

- ✓ "To Whom Am I Speaking?" "Paper Arguments" and "Back Talk" (pages 99-101)
- ✓ paper
- ✓ pencils

I am so excited about summer camp.

Get Ready

Discuss dialogue with the children, both in terms of function and form.

We use dialogue to move along the action in a story and to show our readers how someone other than our main character is feeling, since we don't have any other way of getting inside this other person's head. Dialogue should be used only if it adds something to the story. It must flow smoothly and have a natural sound. (Ironically, this doesn't mean writing the way people speak. Normal conversation is full of unfinished sentences, incomplete thoughts and interruptions, but this kind of speech is too hard to follow and too lengthy for a story.) And remember, each time a new character speaks, you must start a new paragraph. If you don't, your reader will become hopelessly confused.

Helpful Hints

- ✓ Avoid using impossible verbs:
    "I wish I were beautiful," sighed Leah.
    "Yeah, right," laughed Kevin.
- ✓ You can't sigh or laugh while you are talking. Instead try:
    "I wish I were rich." Leah sighed.
    "Yeah, right," said Kevin and burst into laughter.

- ✓ Avoid using adverbs in your dialogue tags. Don't have your characters "laugh happily" or "sob sadly." You can be pretty sure that a laughing person is happy and a sobbing person is sad. If your verb doesn't seem clear or specific enough without the adverb, try a different verb–one that is more precise: "giggled" or "chortled"; "wept" or "bawled."

- ✓ It is easy to overwork the word said in dialogue. Alternatives can be used sparingly–*replied, answered, asked, wondered, exclaimed, screamed, shouted* and *whispered*–but overuse can make your writing sound stilted and artificial. *Said* is often the best choice. If the dialogue is moving along well, chances are your reader won't notice the repetition.
    - Sometimes, it is not even necessary to use a dialogue tag. In a conversation between two people, the way each character speaks and/or the content of his speech are identification enough (a). Even an action that follows a piece of dialogue can be used to show rather than tell the reader who is speaking (b).
    a) "I don't think so," said Michael, turning his back on David.
    "Oh yeah?" cried David, grabbing Michael by the shoulders and spinning him around.
    "Yeah!"
    "Well you're wrong!"
    "Prove it!"
    "I don't have to prove anything to you!"
    "You do if you want me to believe it."
    "Fine. Don't believe me; I don't care." David turned and walked away.
    "Wait!" said Michael.
    b) "You are a pig-headed know-it-all, Thomas, and everyone thinks so!" Andrea threw their project on the floor and ran out of the room.

- ✓ Each character in a story should speak in a distinctive way. Once readers get to know your characters, they should be able to tell who is talking just by what they are saying or how they are saying it. One reader might be aggressive and speak his or her mind freely and often. Another might be shy and hesitant in speech. Someone might not be able to help criticizing others, while another can't stop apologizing. The way your characters talk will reflect their personalities and identify them to the reader.

To Whom Am I Speaking?

What to Do

1. Share and discuss the example below. (In a story, there would be less talk and more action. The characters would be doing as much or more showing as they are telling. This exercise, and the two that follow, are designed to create an artificial environment in which kids are introduced to the mechanics of dialogue and are free to experiment with paper conversations.)
2. Have the children write their own dialogue between two people.
3. Allow only two dialogue tags: one for each of the speakers. (These will probably appear after each person's first line of speech.) The rest of the dialogue should be left untagged.
4. Ask the children to read their conversations aloud. Can you tell who is speaking just by what is said and how?

Example:
"Okay. I'll do it," agreed Marcie.
"Are you sure?" asked Eric.
"Yes. I'm sure."
"It'll probably be scary."
"I can handle it."
"One of us might even get hurt."
"Fine . . . as long as it's you."
"What made you change your mind?"
"I don't know. I guess I just don't want you going around telling everyone that I'm a coward."
"Aw, come on, Marcie. You know me better than that. I don't kiss and tell."
"Yeah, right. What about Paul?"
"Paul deserved it."
"Paul was a coward like me."
"Not like you."
"Why not?"
"Paul didn't agree to do it."
"You see what I mean? You're a cruel and heartless beast."
"I know. Isn't it great?"

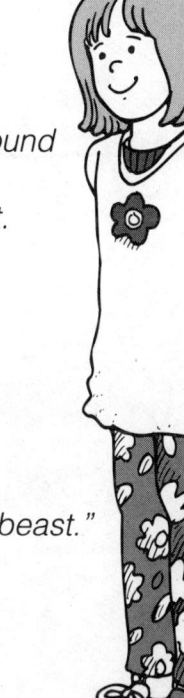

Paper Arguments

What to Do

1. Share and discuss the example.
2. Ask the children to write a paper argument between two friends.
3. Make sure that all dialogue is in quotation marks and that each speaker gets his own paragraph. Dialogue tags are optional.
4. Share the arguments out loud. Do they sound convincing? Would people really argue like that?

Example:

"Alex, give it back."

"Give what back?"

"My math book."

"Your math book?"

"Don't play dumb, Alex, I know you took it."

"I did not take your math book, Daniel."

"Well, if you didn't take it, then who did?"

"How do I know?"

"And if you didn't take it, how come you were looking inside my desk this morning?"

"I was looking for an eraser."

"You were looking for my math book . . . and I guess you found it."

"You're crazy, Daniel."

"I may be crazy, but you're a thief!"

"I am not a thief!"

"You stole my math book so that makes you a thief."

"Daniel, I am going to say this one last time. I did not take your stupid math book. Why don't you ask Sarah where it is? I saw her rifling your desk at lunchtime."

"Okay, I will."

"Fine."

Back Talk

What to Do

1. Share and discuss the example below.
2. Ask the children to write a short conversation between two friends who are talking about a third. Make sure they include some descriptive dialogue tags.
3. Read the conversations out loud. Do they work?

   Example:

   "Boy, is Jane ever lucky," said Susie with envy.

   "Why?" asked Judy.

   "Haven't you heard?"

   "Heard what?" Judy asked, eyes wide with curiosity.

   "About Jane's new car."

   "Jane has a new car?" cried Judy in disbelief.

   "Where have you been, girl?" said Susie. "Everyone's talking about it."

   "I've been in Bermuda. Where do you think?" said Judy, deflating a little, her voice thick with sarcasm. "Now tell me about Jane's car."

   "She got it for her eighteenth," said Susie, mimicking Jane's voice.

   "Her eighteenth birthday?" asked Judy.

   "No, her eighteenth boyfriend, stupid. Of course her eighteenth birthday!"

   "A car for her birthday?" cried Judy, ignoring Susie's dig. "She can't even drive yet!"

   "I know. She's so spoiled," said Susie. "I bet her parents just bought it so they could show everyone how stinking rich they are."

   "Well I think a car's a stupid gift," summed up Judy with a snort.

   "Oh, yeah? Why's that?"

   "Because I would sooner have a van!"

All Good Things Must Come to an End

Getting stopped is often just as hard–or harder–than getting started, but all good stories must come to an end. In this exercise, children learn how to bring their writing to a satisfying and logical conclusion.

Materials

✓ one or more unfamiliar short stories
✓ paper
✓ pencils

Get Ready

Talk about the words *The end* and what it means to bring a story to a logical conclusion.

Endings can be happy or sad, but they must make sense and satisfy the reader. Even if the ending was unexpected or unwanted, the reader must feel that it tied the story up neatly. This means that the main character must have solved his problems and undergone some kind of personality change in the process. There should be no loose ends lying around–even if a sequel is in the works! The ending doesn't have to be predictable, although many are. Surprises are fine as long as the writer has built an element of suspense into her story.

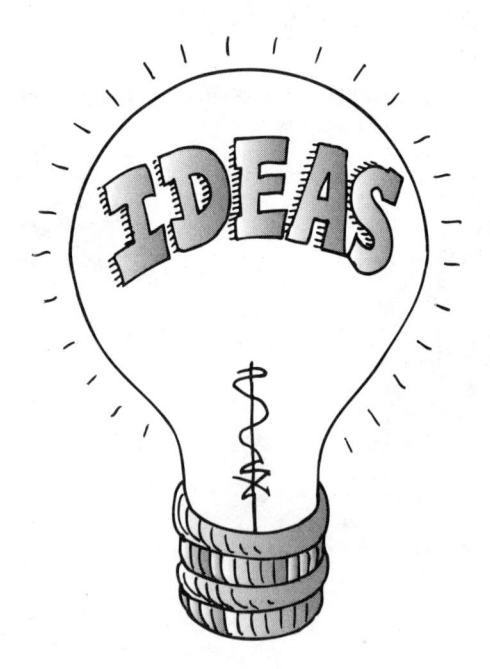

When writing a story, it is important to try a few different endings. You'll know when you have hit on the right one: that little voice inside your head will say "YES!" not "so what?" Test your intuition and the effectiveness of your ending by going through the checklist on page 103. And remember: no "cop-out" endings such as mass executions or "it was all a dream."

What to Do

1. Read an unfamiliar short story to the class. Leave off the ending.
2. Have each child write his own ending to the story.
3. To make sure the ending is appropriate, have each child ask herself the following questions:
   - Has the main character resolved his or her conflict?
   - Does the ending fizzle out or end with a bang?
   - Have I left any important questions unanswered?
   - Would I want to read this story?
4. Compare the faux endings as a class. Which one feels the most satisfying?
5. Read the real ending. Which faux ending was closest? Are yours better?

Try This

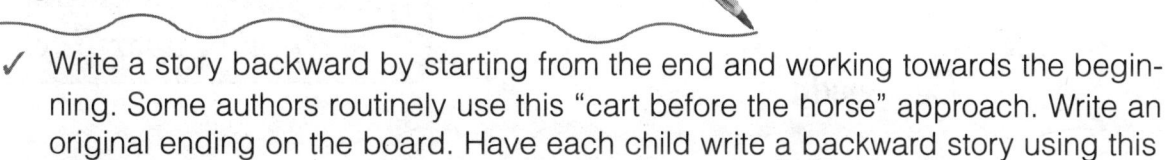

✓ Write a story backward by starting from the end and working towards the beginning. Some authors routinely use this "cart before the horse" approach. Write an original ending on the board. Have each child write a backward story using this ending. Share the stories aloud. How similar/dissimilar are they?

Title Tricks

People often pick up a book because they find the title appealing. In this naming game, kids learn how to come up with meaningful, catchy titles that grab–and hold–a reader's attention.

Materials

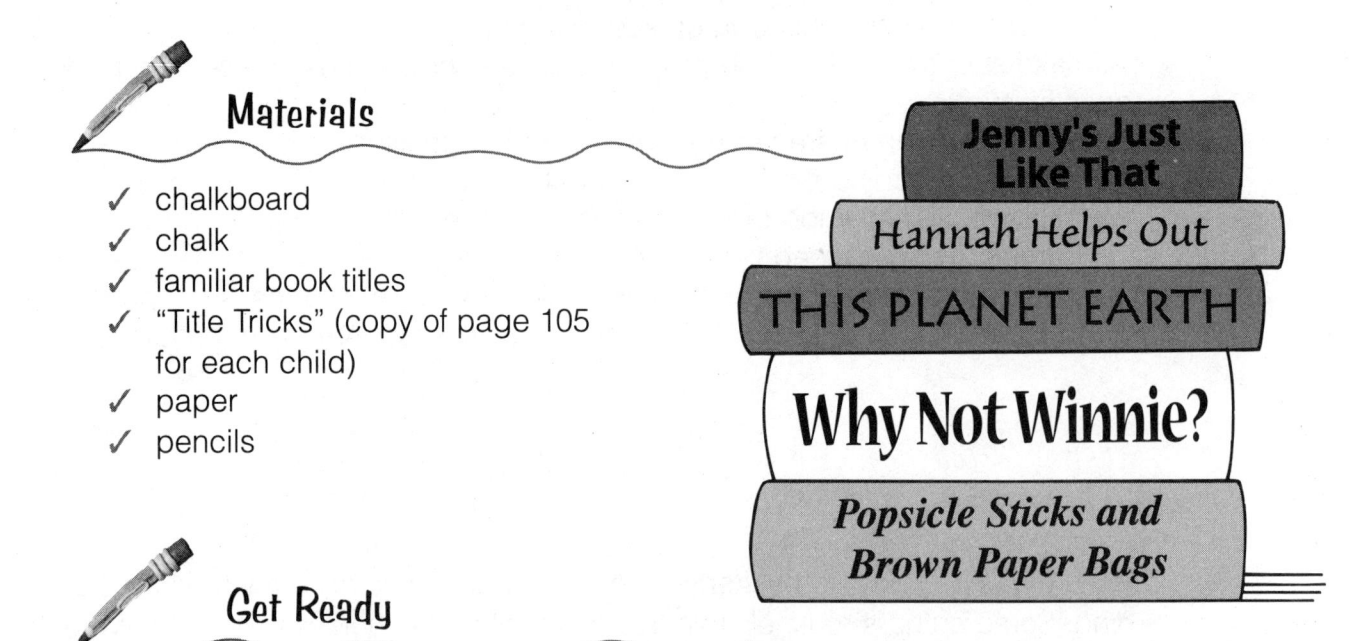

- chalkboard
- chalk
- familiar book titles
- "Title Tricks" (copy of page 105 for each child)
- paper
- pencils

Jenny's Just Like That
Hannah Helps Out
THIS PLANET EARTH
Why Not Winnie?
Popsicle Sticks and Brown Paper Bags

Get Ready

Discuss the importance and function of titles.

Titles should be catchy or interesting and should mean something to the reader. They should say something about the story, often giving the reader a clue about what is going to happen. Titles often come after a story is written, but when they come first they are inspirational!

Ginnys Gumdrop Bugs . . .
Casey Captures Summer's Blooms . . .
When the Wind Sings . . .
Summers I Remember . . .

Title Tricks

✓ **Alliteration:** Using words that start with the same sound in a title:
Dropout Davie or *The Trouble with Tarantulas* or *Wrong-Way Robbie* or *Hannah Helps Out*

✓ **Questions:** Using a question as a title:
Not Again? or *Going My Way?* or *Why Not Winnie?* or *Is This Your Elephant?*

✓ **Statements:** Using a simple statement for a title:
Just Like Last Time or *It Happens Every February* or *Something Evil Lives at Our House* or *Jenny's Just Like That*

✓ **Events:** Using an occurrence or event as a title:
The Peanut Butter Caper or *Margaret's Big Mistake* or *Alone on a Mountaintop* or *Baby Cleans Up*

✓ **Nouns:** Using people, places or things as the focus of a title:
The Magic Slipper or *This Planet Earth* or *The Really Big Wind* or *A Boy Named Hiroshima*

✓ **Crazy Combinations:** Combining words that don't normally go together in a title:
Popsicle Sticks and Brown Paper Bags or *Dancing with Dynamite* or *Pizza and Arcade Games* or *Fireworks, Friends and Fugitives*

✓ **Point/Counterpoint:** Using contradiction in a title:
You Go Your Way, I'll Go Mine or *Right Again, Wrong Again* or *One Step Forward and Two Steps Back* or *Up, Down and Sideways*

✓ **Dialogue:** Using dialogue as a title:
"I Hate You, Joe Kriger!" or *"Leave Me Alone!"* or *"Not This Time, Katy"* or *"Not Now, I'm Busy"*

What to Do

1. Write the titles of some familiar books on the board. Talk about what they represent, how they relate to the book and why they work (or don't work).
2. Discuss each of the title tricks described on the previous page.
3. Write some examples on the board. (Note that title tricks can be combined: alliteration can be combined with a question or an oddity.)
4. As a class, create a number of new titles for each trick.
5. Referring back to the familiar book titles, have the children create at least one new title for each book using a trick from the list.
6. Ask the children to create their own catchy titles using each one of the title tricks.
7. Share these titles as a class.
8. Have the children write (at least) the beginning of a story using one of their own catchy titles as inspiration.

Try This

✓ After writing a story, have the children apply this checklist to their titles:
- Is the title appropriate for the audience?
- Does the title include a key word or phrase from your story? If so, is it a catchy or interesting one?
- Will the title grab the reader's attention?
- What is the "hook?" (the thing that will draw your reader in)
- Is there another story out there with the same name?
- Do other people like the title? Does it make them want to read the story?

Chapter 6

Let's Have Some Fun

Come to Your Senses

In this extremely challenging activity, children push their descriptive abilities by scrambling their senses and creating intriguing sentences that are filled with vivid imagery.

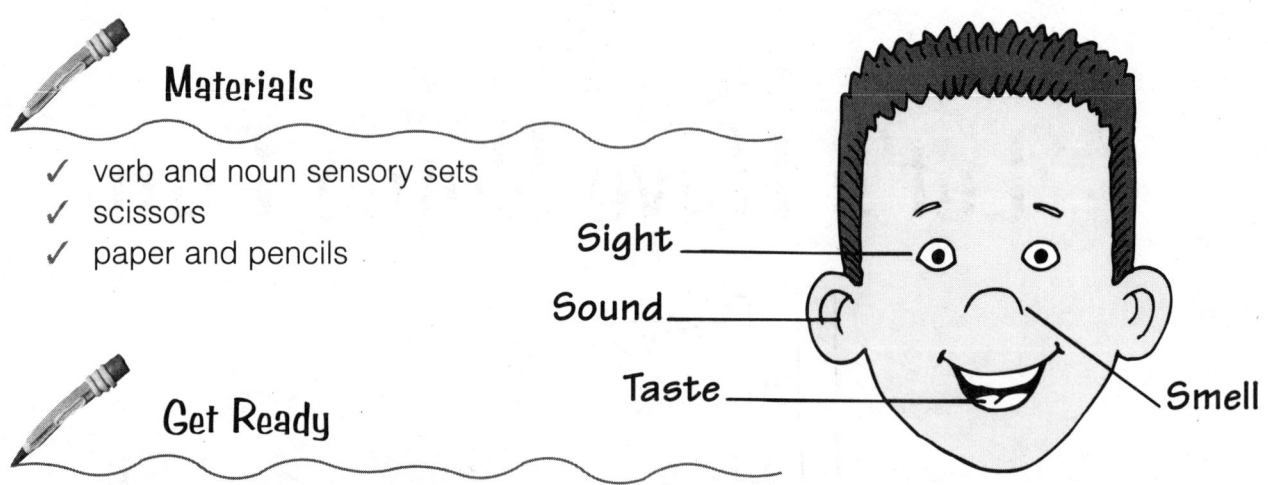

Materials

✓ verb and noun sensory sets
✓ scissors
✓ paper and pencils

Get Ready

Discuss the five senses: touch, taste, see, smell and hear.

In normal writing, we touch things with our bodies, we taste things with our mouths, we see things with our eyes, we smell things with our noses and we hear things with our ears.

But what if we mixed up our senses? What if, for example, we could see a sound, hear a smell, taste a feeling, smell a sight or touch a taste? Our writing would be filled with vivid imagery. Read the following examples aloud. See if the children can figure out how the senses have been scrambled.

a) And as I watched, the howling wind clawed its fingers through the crack in my window and snatched the air from my lungs to fuel itself. *(See a sound.)*

b) The heady perfume of his pine-bough sanctuary sang in his ears like a choir of angels. *(Hear a smell.)*

c) His anger tasted bitter on his tongue. *(Taste a feeling.)*

d) The dancing flames smelled like death. *(Smell a sight.)*

e) Like a treasure too dear to surrender, he clutched the sweet taste of this last berry in his starving hands and refused to let go. *(Touch a taste.)*

What to Do

1. Cut two long strips of paper.
2. On one strip, print the five senses: touch, taste, see, hear and smell. This is the verb set.
3. On the other strip, print the words *feel, taste, sight, sound* and *smell*. This is the noun set.
4. Cut the strips so that you have two sensory card sets: the verb set and noun set.
5. Place the sets facedown in two separate piles and shuffle.
6. Draw one card from each pile.
7. Place the verb and noun cards side by side.
8. Have the children write a sentence that will satisfy the verb/noun combination on the cards. (For example: if the verb card reads *touch* and the noun card reads *sight*, the children will have to create a sentence in which they "touch" a "sight." If two matching sensory cards are drawn, the job will be easy!)
9. Ask the children to read some of their sentences out loud.
10. Reshuffle and draw again.

Try This

✓ Describe a feeling using all five senses.

Anger (the feeling) is a black train, hurtling through a moonless night. (sight) It tastes like acid on my tongue (taste) and sears my nostrils with its pungent burnt-wood smell. (smell) It screeches in my eardrums like fingernails on a chalkboard. (hearing) Anger feels like the spent sulfur of a blown-out match. It stains my soul with its crisp, black powder. (touch)

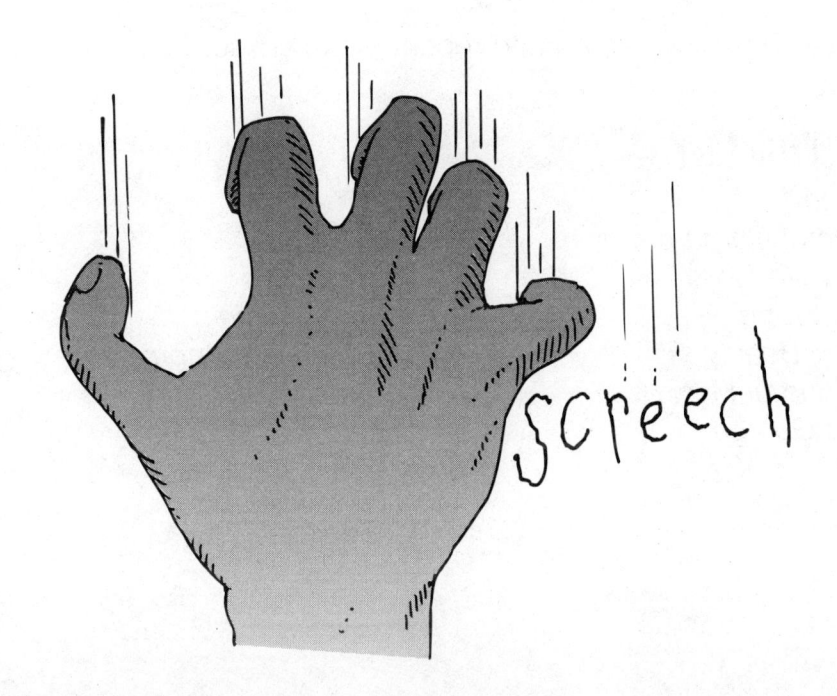

The Movie Name Game

In this story starter activity, children use familiar movie titles as the context for their creative writing.

Materials

- chalkboard or flip chart
- chalk or markers
- paper
- pencils

What to Do

1. As a group, brainstorm to come up with at least 10 different movie titles.
2. Write each of these on the chalkboard or chart.
3. Have the children write the beginning (or all) of a story that incorporates every one of the movie titles listed on the board. *(The titles are not to be used as titles but as parts of sentences within the body of the story! See the Movie Title List and Story below and on the next page.)*

Try This

- Develop a song title list and repeat the exercise.

Movie Title List

Madeline
The Secret Garden
Snow White
The Lion King
Sleeping Beauty
The Sound of Music
Curious George

Babe
Black Beauty
The Rescuers
Fly Away Home
The Sorcerer's Apprentice
The Black Cauldron

Madeline's Magic

A Movie Title Story Starter by Tracey Ann Schofield

With one last glance over her shoulder, Madeline slipped into the secret garden. Snow-white lilies nodded their heads at her arrival. George, her fat black cat, was already there: the lion king, unconcerned, unaware and asleep on duty as usual.

"Wake up, you lazy sleeping beauty," chastised Madeline gently as she tickled beneath his chin. "You're supposed to be guarding our secret."

The sound of music, almost obscured by the rumble of pleasure George was emitting from deep in his throat, drifted over walls of the garden.

"Listen, George. The party is starting without us. We haven't much time."

Madeline scooped the cat into her arms and made her way through a tangle of shrubbery to the center of the garden. There, on a crumbling pedestal, stood a gleaming black cauldron.

"Isn't it magnificent, George?" She was never prepared for the mysterious black beauty of the cauldron–or the absolute silence that enveloped them in the heart of the thicket. Today, however, the quiet was punctured by a tiny, repeating sound that echoed from the depths of the great pot.

Curious, George sat at the base of the pedestal and tilted his head from side to side. He looked at Madeline as if to say, "The cauldron has never spoken before."

Madeline approached the pedestal cautiously and peered inside.

"Well I never!" she cried, reaching down into the darkness and lifting out a small, squawking body in her cupped hands. "It's a wee bird, George. A babe! It must have fallen from its nest!"

As if to confirm the girl's suspicions, a cacophony of chirps erupted in the branches above them.

George sat at attention and began to twitch his tail.

"Now, George. Mind your manners. We're the rescuers today."

"Does this belong to you?" Madeline asked the agitated parent birds as she stood on her tiptoes and pushed the baby up into the shady green of the tree. She was answered with a rush of frantic flapping and leaf rustling.

"He does? Well, then. Go on little fellow. Fly away home to your family."

The baby fluttered its flightless wings and was lost in the foliage. A few delighted chirps later, utter stillness and silence returned to the thicket.

"Well, George. That was a pretty good disappearing act," said Madeline, brushing a few tiny feathers from her hands–all that was left of the bird. "Not bad for the little witch-in-training and the sorcerer's apprentice!"

"George?"

But the cat was gone.

"Well, well, well!" cackled Madeline as she patted the black cauldron affectionately. "I guess we're better than I thought!"

Let's Do Lunch

For this special event, children are invited to eat lunch at school– and enjoy some special brown bag reading and writing activities while they munch.

Here are some Lunch Bag Luncheon ideas to try at your party. Make sure you send the invitation home well in advance, and don't forget to find out if any of your students have food allergies. Have fun!

Tell-a-Tale Time
Have each child bring in one of his favorite stories to share with the class. Each student should be prepared to give a brief summary of the story, discuss why it is a favorite, show some special pictures and read a key paragraph. (Depending on the time, some or all these stories can be read aloud to the class.)

Swap Shop
To play this mystery exchange game, each child must write three clues on a slip of paper about the treat he wishes to offer for trade. (A chocolate chip cookie, for example, could be put up for trade with the following clues: It's crunchy. It's flat. It has brown polka dots.) Have the children exchange slips with a friend. Each partner has to correctly guess the identity of his or her mystery treat before he or she can make the trade. (Try this as a group activity. If a child gets stuck, let the others–but not the clue writer–help out.)

Taster's Choice
Have each child select and sample one lunch item. Then ask him to describe the way the item tastes for the rest of the members of the group. (Descriptions can be as long or as short as the child desires.)
- ✓ Try this as a mystery activity. Have the children take turns wearing a blindfold, and then sample and describe a food item from another child's lunch.

Swell Sell Snack Auction

In this quick-paced, high-stakes sales game, children get to pitch their own snacks and use their profits to purchase others. Before opening up the floor to your "Snack Salespeople," give each child five paper money tokens. Ask the children to come up with a delicious description for a snack they wish to offer for "sale." (For example, a brownie could be pitched like this: "Let me tell you about this little piece of heaven on Earth. Made by the sweetest hands this side of the Mississippi, this sumptuous treat has graced the tea table of the Queen of England herself. Fit for royalty, yet miraculously for sale here today, I offer you the most delicate, decadent, delicious melt-in-your-mouth chocolate brownie the likes you have ever had the good fortune to savor.") Hand out numbers to determine the order of the sales pitches. (You should be the last to make your pitch.) The more irresistible the sales pitch, the more the child can command for his snack. And the more the child commands for her snack, the more she will earn to bid on another. The bidding continues until each child has had the opportunity to buy and sell one snack.

Today's Special and The Ultimate Lunch Menu

Today's Special
Print *Today's Special* at the top of a number of long strips of paper (one for each child) and divide each strip into four sections: Appetizer, Entree, Dessert and Drink. Have children list the items in their lunch under the appropriate heading and print a brief description beside each.

The Ultimate Lunch Menu
Pass out menu boards (11" x 17" [28 x 43 cm] sheets of paper folded in the middle) to each child. Individually or as a group, have children create their "Ultimate Lunch Menu." Each exotic menu item–appetizers, entrees, desserts and drinks–should be accompanied by a delicious description and a price. For example, encourage creativity–even craziness! Think up names for a restaurant that would offer such a magnificent menu!

Brown Bag Story Builders

In this cooperative activity, children build stories on brown paper bags.
- ✓ Divide into small groups. Have one child start the story by writing an opening sentence on the bag and then passing it to the next person. This child must build the story by adding another sentence. The children take turns adding to the story and passing the bag until the tale is complete.

Sandwich Stories

- ✓ Copy "Sandwich Story" cut-outs (see below and on page 115) onto colored paper. There should be enough cut-outs for every child to have a complete set. (The bread slice must be copied twice for each child. One slice will be used for the cover page, the other reserved for "The end.")
- ✓ Have the children write a short story individually or as a group (see Story Builders on page 77) or re-create a familiar one.
- ✓ Have children print the title on one slice of bread, the words *The end* on the other, and the body of the story on the other sandwich ingredients. (Keen writers can be given extra "ingredients" to make another Sandwich Story at home.)
- ✓ Staple the pages together for one yummy story!

Sandwich Story

115

Hey, kids...
let's do lunch!

On _____

our class is having a Brown Bag Luncheon
and you're invited!

Bring your lunch to school, and we'll play some great games while we eat.

Crunch and munch to these brown bag party classics
- ✓ Tell-a-Tale Time
- ✓ Swap Shop
- ✓ Swell Sell Snack Auction
- ✓ The Ultimate Lunch
- ✓ Taster's Choice
- ✓ Brown Bag Story Builders
- ✓ Sandwich Stories

Make sure you bring a favorite story and a few extra goodies to share with your friends.

Can't wait to see you there!

(Hey. This could turn into an all-afternoon affair!)

Yours in lunchtime fun,

Appendix

Grade 4 Writing Assessment Form

Name _____

Expectations	Achievement Level	Comments
Understanding, Spelling and Usage of Words		
has developed a sight vocabulary appropriate for grade level		
uses a variety of strategies to decipher and spell unfamiliar words		
uses proper resources to check spelling		
uses prefixes and suffixes, compound words, synonyms and antonyms		
Use of Writing		
expresses ideas and information with clarity of written expression		
plans information to convey a clear message		
organizes information into paragraphs		
communicates ideas through a variety of simple writing forms		
revises, edits, proofreads and corrects simple pieces of writing		
brings experience and knowledge of the outside world to written work		
demonstrates creativity in written works		

Grade 4 Writing Assessment Form continued

Expectations	Achievement Level	Comments
Grammar and Punctuation		
uses correct verb tenses		
composes effective simple and compound sentences using nouns, verbs, adjectives and adverbs correctly		
demonstrates proper use of the capital letter, period, question mark, comma, exclamation mark, apostrophe and quotation mark		
revises, edits and proofreads work		
Visual Presentation		
demonstrates legible printing and cursive writing		
uses space, headings and paragraph form to enhance presentation		
enhances visual presentation with various forms of media		
analyzes visual messages and materials presented		

Grade 4 Writing Assessment Form continued

Expectations	Achievement Level	Comments
Oral Communication		
draws on a rich vocabulary		
uses tone and gestures to convey, enhance information		
gives an effective brief oral presentation		
relays information in an organized manner		
listens and discusses		

Achievement Level Key
1. Demonstrates independent, consistent mastery of skill or understanding of concept.
2. Demonstrates mastery of skill or understanding of concept most of the time.
3. Demonstrates a limited mastery of skill or understanding of concept with assistance.
4. Needs further assistance to acquire skill or understand concept.

Grade 5 Writing Assessment Form

Name _____

Expectations	Achievement Level	Comments
Understanding and Usage of Print		
makes use of a sight vocabulary appropriate for grade level		
brings new vocabulary from other subject areas to written work		
utilizes a variety of strategies and recall of rules and exceptions to spell unfamiliar words		
uses proper resources to check spelling and grammar		
makes use of specific language and tone for specific purposes		
Use of Writing		
expresses ideas and information with clarity of written expression for a variety of purposes		
makes use of a variety of simple, compound and complex sentences		
organizes information into a series of effective paragraphs		
communicates ideas through a variety of writing forms		
revises, edits, proofreads and corrects written works		
makes use of proper resources to check grammar and spelling		
demonstrates creativity in written works		
brings experience and knowledge of the outside world to written work		

Grade 5 Writing Assessment Form continued

Expectations	Achievement Level	Comments
Grammar and Punctuation		
uses correct noun-pronoun agreement		
uses nouns, verbs, adjectives and adverbs correctly		
demonstrates proper use of capital letters, periods, question marks, commas, exclamation marks, apostrophes and quotation marks		
Visual Presentation		
has mastered cursive writing		
uses space, headings, graphs, labels and captions to enhance presentation		
uses a variety of artistic mediums to enhance visual presentation		
analyzes visual messages and materials presented		

Grade 5 Writing Assessment Form continued

Expectations	Achievement Level	Comments
Oral Communication		
draws on a grade-appropriate vocabulary		
uses tone and gestures to enhance information		
presents in a clear, effective manner		
relays information in an organized manner		
listens and contributes well in discussions		
listens and responds effectively in problem-solving situations		

Achievement Level Key
1. Demonstrates independent, consistent mastery of skill or understanding of concept.
2. Demonstrates mastery of skill or understanding of concept most of the time.
3. Demonstrates a limited mastery of skill or understanding of concept with assistance.
4. Needs further assistance to acquire skill or understand concept.

Grade 6 Writing Assessment Form

Name _____

Expectations	Achievement Level	Comments
Understanding and Usage of Print		
makes use of a sight vocabulary appropriate for grade level		
brings new vocabulary from other subject areas to written work		
utilizes a variety of strategies and recall of rules and exceptions to spell unfamiliar words		
uses proper resources to check spelling and grammar		
makes use of specific language and tone for specific purposes		
Use of Writing		
expresses ideas and information with clarity of written expression for a variety of purposes		
makes use of a variety of simple, compound and complex sentences		
organizes information into a series of effective paragraphs		
communicates ideas through a variety of writing forms		
revises, edits, proofreads and corrects written works		
makes use of proper resources to check grammar and spelling		
demonstrates creativity in written works		
brings experience and knowledge of the outside world to written work		

Grade 6 Writing Assessment Form continued

Expectations	Achievement Level	Comments
Grammar and Punctuation		
uses correct noun-pronoun agreement		
uses nouns, verbs, adjectives and adverbs correctly		
demonstrates proper use of capital letters, periods, question marks, commas, exclamation marks, apostrophes and quotation marks		
Visual Presentation		
has mastered cursive writing		
uses space, headings, graphs, labels and captions to enhance presentation		
uses a variety of artistic mediums to enhance visual presentation		
analyzes visual messages and materials presented		

Grade 6 Writing Assessment Form continued

Expectations	Achievement Level	Comments
Oral Communication		
draws on a grade-appropriate vocabulary		
uses tone and gestures to enhance information		
presents in a clear, effective manner		
relays information in an organized manner		
listens and contributes well in discussions		
listens and responds effectively in problem-solving situations		

Achievement Level Key
1. Demonstrates independent, consistent mastery of skill or understanding of concept.
2. Demonstrates mastery of skill or understanding of concept most of the time.
3. Demonstrates a limited mastery of skill or understanding of concept with assistance.
4. Needs further assistance to acquire skill or understand concept.

Writing Tips for Aspiring Authors

- ✓ Write creatively every day–even for a few minutes. Write two sentences about how you're feeling. Add adjectives to a shopping list. Create a creepy character. Describe your bedroom. Write a poem. Anything! Just write.

- ✓ Practice, practice, practice. If you don't write, you won't get better. Even if you're pretty good at it, keep practicing. It is a craft, and with a craft there is always room for improvement and growth. You may be a great hockey player, but if you don't practice, you'll never make it to the NHL.

- ✓ Write about what you know.

- ✓ Don't overanalyze your work. All writing is good writing.

- ✓ Don't throw anything away! Keep all your writing in a journal, writing notebook or accordion file. You never know when an old idea might work perfectly in a new story. (By the time you're an adult, you'll have forgotten what it is like to be a kid. If you want to write for children, your old "kid feelings" will be indispensable.)

- ✓ Be a sponge. Soak up everything. A conversation you overheard today could very well come up years from now in your writing.

- ✓ Take an ordinary situation, and ask yourself "What if . . ."

- ✓ Imitate. Find a style of writing that you like and copy it. It's not plagiarism; it is a great study habit. We are all influenced by somebody else. Write what you like to read and your own unique style will develop naturally.

- ✓ Write for yourself. Keep your school work and your creative work separate. And don't write because you want to be a published author. Getting published is a great dream but a poor goal. Write because you have terrific words, thoughts and stories in your head. Write because you need to express yourself. You don't have to be published to be a writer. All you have to do is write.

- ✓ Share your work. It is a great way to grow and develop (and to get a little praise and encouragement along the way). Join a writers' group and share your work with people who share your passion.

- ✓ Have fun! Creative writing is supposed to be a leisure activity, not a job.

Answer Key

Synonym Sound-Alikes, page 33

1. arrive alive
2. enter center
3. bad dad
4. fighting writing
5. cruel jewel
6. found ground
7. bright light
8. good hood
9. new shoe
10. alright plight
11. cool pool
12. towards awards
13. quiet riot
14. sell well
15. play today

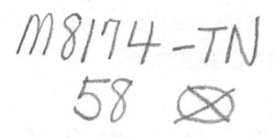